D0645123

THE LAST
LAUGH

Other books by Raymond A. Moody, Jr.

Life After Life: The Investigation of a Phenomenon—
Survival of Bodily Death

The Light Beyond

Reflections on Life After Life

Coming Back:
A Psychiatrist Explores Past-Life Journeys

Scrying: A Feminine Form of Divination

Laugh After Laugh:
The Healing Power of Humor

Life Before Life:
Regression into Past Lives

Audiocassette

Finding the Light

THE LAST
LAUGH

a new philosophy of near-death experiences,
apparitions, and the paranormal

RAYMOND A. MOODY, JR., PH.D., M.D.

HAMPTON ROADS
PUBLISHING COMPANY, INC.
for the evolving human spirit

Copyright © 1999
by Raymond Moody, Jr., M.D., Ph.D.

All rights reserved, including the right to reproduce this
work in any form whatsoever, without permission
in writing from the publisher, except for brief passages
in connection with a review.

Cover design by Marjoram Productions
Cover photo by Jonathan Friedman

For information write:

Hampton Roads Publishing Company, Inc.
134 Burgess Lane
Charlottesville, VA 22902

Or call: 804-296-2772
FAX: 804-296-5096
e-mail: hrpc@hrpub.com
Web site: http://www.hrpub.com

If you are unable to order this book from your local
bookseller, you may order directly from the publisher.
Quantity discounts for organizations are available.
Call 1-800-766-8009, toll-free.

Library of Congress Catalog Card Number: 98-71589

ISBN 1-57174-106-2

10 9 8 7 6 5 4 3 2 1

Printed on acid-free recycled paper in Canada

Table of Contents

PREFACE

Much of what we regard today as New Thought, and nearly all of our most recent constructions and ideas about life after
death, the eternality of the soul, and so-called near-death experiences (NDEs), has been placed in the modern lexicon—has
become possible to even consider—because of the groundbreak-
ing and daring work of one man: Dr. Raymond Moody.

The myriad contributions of others notwithstanding,
Raymond Moody stands as a pioneer in this field, a paver of
ways, a leader—never a follower—on the path. This is, no
doubt, because Dr. Moody is such a profound thinker, and
because he has been willing to generously share his mental
explorations with us—regardless of the consequences.

One has to be willing to have one's ideas labeled folly
before they can be termed insightful, it would seem. Or, as
Shaw put it, all great truths begin as blasphemy. So here comes
more blasphemy from Raymond Moody.

I am not surprised. He has blasphemed before, if blas-
pheming is to call into question our "conventional wisdom";
and, given that definition, he is no doubt going to blaspheme
again.

In this particular volume, the latest work from one of our
most astute scientists, Dr. Moody not only questions conventional ideas, he questions his own very unconventional ones. Of
course, all great scientists do that. They never take anything at
face value, never accept as "finished" any exploration, and never
assume any "proof" to be final. Bravo, then. For they place us
in the challenging position of having to listen to them question

themselves, and because so much of what we believe about our world and our lives has to do with what they, themselves, told us before, we are challenged at more levels than might be, at first, apparent. The biggest challenge, of course, is for us to remain open to others, but, in the end, to do our own thinking.

Many people—millions—actually accepted Raymond Moody's "findings" about near-death experiences and extrapolated from them to produce an entire cosmology about life after death, only now to find that Dr. Moody himself never intended to give us an answer about life after death and other things paranormal, but merely sought to reopen the question.

Now, in the startling treatise that follows, he gets to do just that, and thus to have "the last laugh." Here he goes again, overturning tables, rocking boats, mooing right in the face of sacred cows.

So beware. Only those with active minds, expandable minds, open minds, may happily tarry here. On the other hand, if you count yourself among those, jump right in, the water's fine. It's hot water, to be sure. Dr. Moody doesn't know where else to place himself, but you'll find it pleasing nonetheless. Maybe even a little amusing, as, clearly, does Raymond.

And for those of you who've been taking all this life after death stuff, as well as life itself, a little seriously . . . let yourself have a good laugh. On yourself.

That's what we all need to do, you know. We all need to laugh a little at ourselves. Then we'll really find wisdom.

Thanks, Raymond, for once again leading the way.

Neale Donald Walsch

INTRODUCTION

In a republican nation, whose citizens are to be led by reason and persuasion and not by force, the art of reasoning becomes of first importance.

Thomas Jefferson

The media don't share Thomas Jefferson's faith in the public's judgment and underlying good sense. They feed us sensational stuff on the pretext that none of us like to think, or can. Publishers load up their books about near-death experiences and other paranormal phenomena with catchy stories they call "case histories." But what do the stories mean? That's where the art of reasoning Jefferson mentioned comes in.

This obligatory addendum to *Life After Life* consists of the thoughts commercial publishers edited out of my works during a twenty-year period. The truth is, in their pursuit of riches and for the sake of sensationalism, publisher-editors hacked so much out of what I wrote that for a long time I haven't recognized myself in those books. The covers that publishers stamp with untruthful exclamations like, "Scientific proof of life after death!" are a constant headache and a continuing source of embarrassment. Hype like that sells books, maybe, but it mangles the credibility of the subject.

The publishers rake in the cash, and I'm the one left to answer to the critics' objections—the very objections I had anticipated and resolved in the passages editors either altered or cut out of what I wrote. You can know that publishers haven't tampered with these words, though, because with *The Last Laugh,* I'm taking my identity back.

Right off the bat, I'm taking the extraordinary measure of annexing the entire contents of the book you are holding in your hands into *Life After Life*. Effective immediately, *The Last Laugh* should be incorporated into the earlier book for all serious purposes of reading, discussion, or scholarship. I'll accept responsibility for *Life After Life* only insofar as it is read and interpreted in the broader context provided by this new, required supplement.

I feel strongly that the media are seriously misleading the public by mismanaging information about near-death experiences and the paranormal. Don't get the impression I'm media-bashing, though. Journalists take what the presumed experts on these subjects say as their source material. The fault lies ultimately with the customary but unsound guidelines of controversy under which the supposed authorities conventionally operate.

The Last Laugh challenges settled thinking about the supernatural. Three discrete sects of true believers have long dominated learned discussion about these things. In what follows, I'm intent on dislodging all three sects from their privileged position by setting out an alternate theory about the nature of the paranormal.

The media typecast me as a parapsychologist. That is a grave mistake, and I'm not going to put up with it anymore.

Parapsychologists masquerade as scientists, alleging they can prove mind-reading, prophetic abilities, or life after death by laboratory techniques or, more generally, by rational procedure. In fact, parapsychologists are pseudo-scientists, which means that they espouse a system of methods and assumptions they erroneously regard as scientific.

I'm not implying they're dishonest, by the way. Mostly, parapsychologists are sincere people, pleasantly optimistic, and likeably naive. I classify them with rhapsodists, pipe dreamers, lotus-eaters, and woolgatherers. Having many of these same character weaknesses or dreamy qualities myself, I find most parapsychologists are easy people to be fond of. But their basic assumptions are seriously in error.

Please be patient, now. Don't rush to judgment and conclude I'm one of the sloppy thinkers who pawn themselves off as skeptics about the paranormal. It's a travesty when they mislabel themselves as "skeptics," a dignified term that has a distinguished place in the history of Western philosophical thought.

Many self-styled skeptics about the paranormal join a fringe social movement that advertises itself as a scientific organization while at the same time underhandedly representing itself as a para-law enforcement agency. Let me emphasize, parenthetically, that I'm not making this up! The members of this social movement call themselves the "sigh cops." Later on, I'll explain what they mean by that and why I spell it that way. For now, suffice it to say first that sigh cops aren't skeptics, but believers in a particular ideology about what knowledge is and how it is acquired, and second, that there are good reasons for believing that their ideology is mistaken.

The Last Laugh is an example of philosophical skepticism about the paranormal. I push skepticism far beyond the limits sigh cops set for their inquiries. By comparison to mine, theirs is a weak-kneed and wimpy approach.

You would think two sides would be enough, but there is a third big, bickering batch of people with a firm, definite opinion about the paranormal. They are the goshawful deadfannies, stiffs, bores, nuisances, uptight dogmatists, broken records, and wet blankets; the fundamentalist Christians, Religious Right, Bible Brigade, "JAY-zus"-Sayers, Brimfire and Hellstoners, Swaggartists, Falwellers, Bakker-Boosters, Pat Robertsonians, or whatever you would call them. Out of politeness, I deem them "funda-Christians." By back-clipping, the nickname kindly avoids calling attention to one of their most conspicuous shortcomings, because it doesn't even mention one of the very qualities in which so many of them are weak or deficient.

Religiously, hell, Satan, and demons are among funda-Christians' pet subjects. Nothing can get you sent hellward faster, in the mind of a funda-Christian, than having a healthy curiosity about the paranormal, or taking a sympathetic interest in it. Funda-Christians enjoy watching demons as much as bird watchers enjoy watching birds. Funda-Christians can pick the demons out of any crowd, but the paranormal is one of many funda-Christians' favorite places for watching demons at work. Funda-Christians see anyone who doesn't kowtow to their ideology as the embodiment of evil.

The funda-Christians have been charging me with demonic espionage ever since I went public with my findings about near-death experiences in 1972. Beautiful, bliss-and-love-filled near-death experiences of a bright light upset funda-Christian experts on the paranormal, because they suspect the light-and-love-filled ones may be Satan conducting an undercover operation. Grim, ghastly, flame-filled, agony-and-suffering-ridden, hellish, near-death experiences, in which the people who almost died toasted in torment, are okay by the funda-Christian authorities, though. The infernally-oriented, Satanically-focused, funda-Christian, near-death experience experts enjoy finding cases of hellish experiences. They can use cases like that for writing knowledgeably about Satan, demons, sinners in torment, and eternal damnation. Some of these men write mighty amusing treatises, and I wholeheartedly recommend their works. Or, as I always advise aspiring students of the paranormal, be sure you brace yourself first by consuming one good logician's dose plus one good humorist's dose of the kind of claptrap funda-Christian authorities on the subject write.

A man named Dr. Ravings, if I recall his name correctly, is a main funda-Christian doctor-expert on near-death experiences. This specialist in close call perdition is on the look out for terrifying, infernal, peri-mortal visions. I'm one of the most enthusiastic fans of Dr. Ravings' writings.

When Dr. Ravings writes about hellish near-death experiences, he ties his words tightly into some of the scariest passages King James ever spent money to get translated. Then Ravings twists his arguments together, loosely, with a couple of stray loops of the Bible Belt. Reading vintage Ravings is, oh, so sweet a pleasure, but how sweet a pleasure it really is, I sadly believe, is something only a handful of fellow academically-trained analytic philosophers can fully appreciate.

There is much Dr. Ravings' ravings leave unanswered, though, so I'm eagerly awaiting future volumes of his work, or perhaps future installments is a better way of phrasing it, since it is from the Luther-position, strictly, that Dr. Ravings reasons, or raves. I'm wondering, for example, what system of classification or notation Dr. Ravings uses when he writes up his funda-Christian research findings, say, "Near-Death Experience, Infernal type, Ravings Score II-C," with so many degrees of hell-fever being registered, or however it is, precisely, that he keeps tab of them. I ask lots of other questions about the funda-Christian near-death experts' theories throughout this book.

I once dreamed I met Dr. Ravings, and it was a frightening experience! In the dream, when I caught sight of him, he was standing there as rigid and starched and stiff as a carved wooden figure of a man of his exact proportions and demeanor would have been, had one of them been standing there in Dr. Ravings' place. As I spotted him, the image flashed into my mind of a wooden advertising statue of a man that looked just like Dr. Ravings, posted at the entrance of a commercial building, positioned there to mark the place as a funeral parlor. Or, as I should say, Dr. Ravings suddenly changed into a stiff, sardonic-looking, wooden statue of himself, standing beside the doorway of a funeral home, and I had a sense the effigy was placed there to advertise the business as a mortuary; after all, it's a dream, and not a real or an actual experience I'm telling here.

Dr. Ravings certainly is one hell of a cardiological theologaster, in my opinion. Not to worry, though. Ravings has a back-up man, theologically, in the form of a little demonological assistant, a twirp of a funda-Christian philosophist on the faculty of an alleged "seminary" somewhere out West, but not literally in the town its name suggests, apparently. So I'm relieved that at least it's not one of those awful "seminaries" where they insist on the words always being taken only in their exact literal meanings.

The funda-Christian pipsqueak's name, as I remember it, is Professor Grootish, and as I am interested in words, I've been meaning to look up that root-word "groot." I haven't found the time yet, so perhaps one of my readers will. I can't recommend the professor's books as highly as I do Ravings', though. True, it is a fine loaf of Bible-baloney Grootish carves for his readers, but it's marred by his abhorrently cavalier attitude toward children's hellish near-death experiences. The professor's writing style is dry as dust, too. Positively stuporific, it is chloroform in print. Specifically, Grootish writes gravely and ponderously in a characteristic idiom of the odium theologicum. However, since the odium theologicum is an essential concept any serious student of near-death experiences must grasp, the professor's book is a must-read anyway, despite being hogwash.

The odium theologicum explains why someone could argue the sound logical case that can be made against the kind of ideological recitations Ravings, Grootish, and their hellmates excel at, and could argue it all the way from the Laws of Thought through the propositional and the predicate calculi and into the Godel theorem, and it still wouldn't do one bit of good. The odium theologicum is the bitter hatred that, proverbially, is characteristic of theological disputes. Ultimately, the bitterness peculiar to religious controversy manifests as an obstinate refusal to continue a discussion. That is, when funda-Christians and other religious extremists are questioned about their ideology, and things get too hot for them logically, they just turn a deaf ear to any further discussion. At that point, they typically get in a suit, affect an attitude of studied superiority, look down their noses at whomever they are arguing with, sniff arrogantly, and sulk away in silence. That response pattern is pathognomonic of the odium theologicum. Anyone who has ever observed the behavior will recognize it from my description.

Now, illogic is one thing, but that distinctive obstinacy of the odium theologicum might put someone who is psychologically-minded in mind of constipation—anal retention! Fundamentally, it's as much a matter of their bad bowels as it is of their bad manners that funda-Christian experts chastise us innocent, pro-paranormal experts by linking us with the devil. When Gravings or Rootish, pardon me, I mean Ravings or Grootish or others like them, pre-curse us to hell, or when they insinuate that we are enlistees in the Satan Corps, it really is subconscious anal trouble that is the matter with them and not, as it appears, conscious malice.

When funda-Christian experts on the paranormal single you out as a presumed Satanic representative, I wonder, are you better off denying it, remaining silent, disputing with your accusers, leveling the same charge back at them, making an appointment with an exorcist? What do you do? Emily Post is silent on the question and the Code Duello is a thing of the past. What sort of response is expected when a funda-Christian suspects someone of covert deviltry? I prefer the method of tickling the funda-Christian experts' demoniacal fancies even further.

Granting, as I am, for the purpose of an argument, that I really am the kind of guy funda-Christians imply I am, why, I shudder when I think what maliciously vexatious hexes and spells I might be casting on Grootish and Ravings and all their kind about now. I'll even go so far as to say that if I am on Satan's side, then I have visited a terrible curse, in advance, on any funda-Christian expert on near-death experiences or the paranormal who ever reads this book beyond the end of the very next paragraph. Indeed, I certify that if I actually am in league with the Devil, then I have made a pact with him specifying that all the legions of hell will inflict horrendous suffering and tribulation on any funda-Christian experts on the paranormal or near-death experiences who read this book a single word past the beginning of the second paragraph following this one, or who get anyone else to read it to them or even to explain it to them in general terms, or who listen to it on an audio tape version.

So, if you think about it for a minute, you'll realize no sincere funda-Christian experts on these subjects could be reading this book a bit further than the word at the beginning of the next paragraph. Anyone who really believes in demons, and who knows anything at all about the devilish things, believes demons can possess people, and make them sick. No funda-Christian experts who take Satan seriously can rationalize their way out of this awkward dilemma with some limp excuse like, "Well, uh, yeah, I did read *The Last Laugh*, because first I talked it over with Brother Swaggart and we prayed about it, and we decided, well, hey, I'm saved anyway, so JAY-zus protected me from the Devil the whole time I was reading it." Excuses like that won't hold water if the funda-Christian experts seriously believe I'm on Satan's team, because sincere believers in demons believe the pestilent things can also get to you through unsaved other people, even close relatives or other loved ones, by calling down troubles and sicknesses on them. Clearly, then, no funda-Christian experts who seriously entertain the notion that I'm in cahoots with demons would run the risk of reading *The Last Laugh.* If they did, they would worry every time their frail, unsaved, eighty-seven-year-old grandmothers or uncles came down with the sniffles, or their little children got a bad rash and fever, fearing that maybe demons were at work afflicting their loved ones on account of the funda-Christian experts having slipped up by reading my new book, even one word past the period at the end of this sentence.

O.K., let's pause for a few moments. . . . Now, everyone reading this can be sure that anything in *The Last Laugh* from here on will not be read by any funda-Christian authorities on the paranormal, so from the beginning of this paragraph onward, dear reader, we'll be able to have a lot of fun at their expense. I know enough about good manners that I wouldn't make fun of the funda-Christian experts to their faces. So I use the idea of the hex-and-curse method as a deceptive way of going around behind the funda-Christian experts' backs so I can make fun of them by getting you, my readers, to laugh at them, just as I do.

Now, you can know my words are reaching you over a secure line, with no funda-Christian experts listening in. Remember, readers, you're in on the joke, so don't tell Ravings or Grootish or any of the funda-Christian experts anything about what's in this book, so we can go on laughing at them, and they won't have any idea what we're hee-hawing and guffawing about. That way, you can show up at their lectures and surprise the funda-Christian experts with the many interesting questions about their positions I raise throughout this book.

It's a good thing no funda-Christian experts will be reading *The Last Laugh,* because if they did, it would get their bowels moving again, I believe. I expect it would cause a hell of a cataclysm in the fundamentalists' fundaments if any of them ever followed my arguments through carefully, because *The*

Last Laugh is nothing less than a complete and utter refutation of their entire funda-Christian ideology. Later on, I conclusively demonstrate that, in order to remain JAY-zusly Correct, funda-Christian ideologues' thoughts and words must, as a logical necessity, ramble outside the boundaries of meaningful language where they lapse, therefore, into literal nonsense.

There is no escape for the parapsychologists or the pseudo-skeptics, either, from their own nets of nonsense. *The Last Laugh* demolishes all three of the standard approaches to the paranormal and erects a better, more comprehensive, and pragmatic system of thinking in their place.

It is possible to make sense of peri-mortal visionary experiences in their bearing on the notion of life after death, but it is not a quick fix. It requires following a fairly lengthy argument and working through a paradox that, psychologically, is difficult to negotiate (though it is easy as pie, logically). Initially, it seems odd, but nonetheless, it's true: The paranormal comes pre-equipped with an under-meaning of humor. Hence, if it is life after death that is at issue, earnest and diligent inquiry about near-death experiences next leads smoothly and plausibly into the closely related subjects of play, humor, and entertainment, which are important subtexts of the paranormal.

Initially, my claim seems bizarre, and establishing it will be tedious, admittedly. I believe that readers who follow my arguments through to their conclusions will arrive at what is, ultimately, a more comprehensive, useful, and satisfying solution of the mysteries of the paranormal than is offered by any of the ready-to-wear theories that dominate the market.

Colleagues will understand that I am inviting rational rebuttal. I hope other scholarly paranormalists will show by logical counter-arguments exactly where and how my reasoning breaks down or goes astray, if it does. I enjoy learning through the process of studying other thinkers' well-reasoned, step-by-step correction of my mistakes.

The Last Laugh is a secession from the encrusted controversy about the paranormal and near-death experiences, not a contribution to it. Some may misinterpret the book as an unkind, ungracious, or hostile measure. Coming from me, an author who has long written sympathetically about the paranormal, it may even seem a disloyal measure. People may think I've had a change of heart.

To the contrary: Friends and family know I aspired to be a humorist from the age of eight. When *Life After Life* first was published, a few of my acquaintances assumed it was another one of my pranks. In 1977, I wrote a book about the relationships between humor and the abnormal aspects of the mind, in the same tone as I now have written a book about the relationships between humor and the paranormal aspects of the mind. Many old friends would swear to all this in a court of sigh law, and they would swear it on a stack of Bibles as high as Jerry Falwell's head, or as Pat Robertson's, whichever gentleman is the taller.

Anyone who reads *Life After Life,* my previous work about humor, and *The Last Laugh* will see that the three volumes dovetail smoothly together. I've tied the arguments of this, the latest volume, so tightly into those of the first one that if anyone could knock the chocks out from under *The Last Laugh,* the rest of *Life After Life* would come crashing down along with it. *The Last Laugh* and *Life After Life* are, therefore, one and the same body of work, take it or leave it, and they will stand or fall together. I feel sure of that.

Raymond A. Moody, Jr.

1

THE EXPERIENCE OF DYING

To journey to the afterlife realm and return may seem an impossible dream, but it is an extraordinary feature of late twentieth-century life. Such adventures have become a commonplace theme of popular culture and an accepted reality of collective consciousness. I have listened to thousands of individuals recount their near-death experiences—tantalizing and inspiring visions they saw as they hovered on the brink of death. Many of them were revived after variable periods of time in cardiac arrest, quite a number of them after their physicians believed them to be dead, or even pronounced them dead.

The accounts these people give are strikingly similar, so much so that we can now say that for the most part their experiences conform to a pattern that includes a number of separable elements. Although not everyone reports every feature of the pattern, almost everyone reports some of them, and a considerable number report all of them.

These people say that at the point at which they almost die, often at the moment their hearts stop beating, they undergo a dramatic change of perspective. They seem to leave their physical bodies behind and float upwards, typically to a point above their bodies, perhaps just below the ceiling of the emergency department or operating room of a hospital, or above the scene of an accident. They can clearly see their own physical bodies below, on a table or in the wreckage of a vehicle, and witness the attempt of medical personnel to resuscitate them.

After a time, they may have the impression that they enter a narrow passageway (often characterized as a dark tunnel) and as they move through it, they see a bright light at the end. As they enter into that brilliant white or golden light, they are permeated and comforted with a sense of love and peace that is beyond description, a feeling of ineffable joy. Often, relatives or other loved ones who have already died are there in that light, as if to greet them and to help them through this transition. They often say that these deceased people seem vitally alive. Loved ones who died years before, decrepit and weakened by illness or by years, appear there in the light, restored to a vibrant youthfulness.

Some become aware of what they take to be a boundary or a limit that demarcates the world of ordinary life from a realm that lies beyond life as we know it. This zone of demarcation, they say, seems energetic and dynamic, and they sense that, were they to cross it, they would not be able to return. Although they cannot describe it in everyday language, some have likened it to a body of water—a lake or a river.

As their near-death experiences progress, these dying people may become aware of a loving, luminous presence, a being of love and light, who conducts them through an extraordinary, panoramic review of their lives. Every detail is revealed in colorful, three-dimensional simultaneity, as the loving presence of light helps them to understand the life that now seems to be coming to completion.

Often by this point they do not wish to go back to their lives, but they are informed by the being of light, or by their loved ones, that it is not their time to die. They must go back; they have things left to accomplish. Or, they may be given a choice: the realm of light, or the lives they have been leading. Almost invariably, these people tell us that the reason they have chosen to return is that they have young children to raise. Left to their own preferences, they would have chosen to stay in the light.

Near-death experiences frequently are transformative. The most common of the positive after-effects on the lives of those who undergo them is that, thereafter, they are assured through a personal adventure that life continues beyond death, so they have no more fear of death. They are also certain that the most important thing we can do with ourselves while alive is to learn how to love.

Interest Increases Dramatically

When I was writing my first book, I was one of the few serious students of this subject. During the decades since my initial research was published in *Life After Life*, however, cardiologists, psychiatrists, pediatricians, anesthesiologists, psychologists, scholars who are experts in the field of religious studies, sociologists, and specialists from numerous other clinical or academic disciplines all around the world have scrutinized the near-death experience. A consensus has emerged among these investigators that—just as I observed in my own research—a common pattern of experience unfolds among a significant proportion of persons as they are dying, at least insofar as we can judge from the reports of those who have survived close encounters with the process.

This discovery has fueled an even more noticeable upswing in the scope of interest in the phenomenon. That interest is now truly global. Near-death experiences have been systematically studied by investigators in the United States, Germany, Italy, France, Japan, Norway, Sweden, Denmark, Britain, Holland, the Czech Republic, and Australia. The popular interest in these findings all over the planet is reflected both in the continuing enormous worldwide sales of books devoted to the subject, and in the international fascination with numerous recent films exploring this theme.

Why do near-death experiences appeal so strongly to so many people, and what does their appeal have to do with their bearing on life after death? What is new, and what comes next, in research into the astonishing peri-mortal visionary experiences that are so common throughout the world?

These are pressing questions, because startling new information is waiting in the wings, further glad tidings from the near beyond that are dormant in what the general public and many qualified professionals and academicians already affirm.

A New Kind of Near-Death Experience

We have now learned that there is a new kind of near-death experience. This has been discovered and confirmed by the same kinds of first-person accounts from trustworthy individuals, and the same kinds of independent investigations by numerous professionals, that have sought to establish that there are near-death experiences of any kind in the first place.

I do not believe this "new type" of near-death experience has been previously reported, or surely not widely so.

The near-death experience with which most of us are now familiar is the experience of a person who almost dies, but does not, and "comes back to life" to tell extraordinary stories about what happened.

The new kind of near-death experience is the experience of a person who is not dying, but who is with another who is dying. I have called this an "empathic near-death experience," shared near-death experience, conjoint near-death experiences, or mutual near-death experience.

I don't know yet just what name is best or most accurate, but whatever this experience is to be called, it is now clear to me that it is very common for someone at the bedside of a person who is dying to participate empathetically in the dying experience of that other person.

Dozens upon dozens of first-rate individuals have related to me that, as a loved one died, they themselves lifted out of their own bodies and accompanied their dying loved ones upward toward a beautiful and loving light. Others have said that, as they sat with their dying loved ones, they perceived deceased relatives coming to greet the one who was passing away.

Those in close attendance at the bedside often are convinced they are participating simultaneously, intuitively, and intimately in the ongoing transcendental experience of the dying. From what I have heard of these shared near-death experiences, they are bringing the same message of the overriding importance of love as did the initial wave of first-person near-death experiences.

Having a close personal attachment to the dying person may increase the likelihood that someone else will have a shared near-death experience, yet that does not seem to be a necessary condition. Lots of doctors and nurses have described to me how they perceived patients' spirits leaving their bodies at the point of death. Helping professionals often have other extraordinary spiritual experiences under those circumstances as well. These statements will be borne out by many other investigators who are physicians, nurses, psychologists, and hospice counselors. In fact, I have already discussed these findings with several other well-known authorities in the field, all of whom agreed from their own professional experience that conjoint near-death experiences are remarkably common.

There are already enough grounded, responsible individuals out there who have shared in the dying experiences of their loved ones to allow any sympathetic, careful, and well-intentioned clinical investigator who desires to do so to be able to confirm what I am claiming.

Indeed, there appears now to be a sudden flood of reports of "shared near-death experiences," and countless people are going through a lot of soul-searching about their personal experiences of this nature. The flood has been caused, no doubt, by the fact that the vast group of Americans known as the baby boomers, however vaguely or precisely that term may be defined, now are coming into the times of their lives in which it is common to lose parents or other dear ones. Nor can it be forgotten that many young persons now are losing others at ages far too young.

Not only are more of us enduring the death of our loved ones, more of us are experiencing their death right in front of our eyes. Customs are no longer what they were a couple of decades ago, when the family at the bedside was shooed out of the room before death actually occurred. Today, relatives are encouraged to be there at the end.

For these reasons, we now have more witnesses to the deaths of loved ones—and a corresponding increase in the opportunities for empathic, or shared, near-death experiences.

Barriers to Acceptance

Sooner or later this additional information about the new kind of near-death experience is bound to come out into the open (as it is doing with this book).

"Shared near-death experiences" are becoming so widespread in the population that virtually anyone who has not had such an experience personally will soon be hearing about it directly from some other trustworthy personal acquaintance or loved one—a wizened Uncle Herman, a beloved parent, a longtime best pal, or a close confidant. Once the volume of this anecdotal data reaches critical mass, it will be virtually impossible to ignore it. Accepting it may be another matter.

Because so much of the latest information about perimortal visionary experiences is of surpassing strangeness, neither the public nor the informed specialists are able to easily accept it. They can listen to it, but they cannot hear it.

What makes the new information "surpassingly strange" is not that it is "strange" in and of itself, but that it falls outside of the currently familiar ways in which most people think about near-death experiences—and all seemingly "paranormal" phenomena. A large part of the first portion of this book is going to be devoted to looking at that, for just this reason.

These familiar, if inaccurate, perspectives—the way most people think about near-death experiences—have their antecedents in very early times, and these perspectives are all fixtures of a continuing debate going back at least two millennia. That debate will go on for the next two millennia if someone or something doesn't break up the logjam.

That's precisely what this book hopes to do.

Just as *Life After Life* broke the silence and opened the floodgates around the topic of near-death experiences of the dying, now *The Last Laugh* seeks to pry open the dam holding back the stream of information about the near-death experiences of those *with* the dying.

Breaking Up the Logjam

It's time we discussed the entire subject. And not just this subject, but the whole topic of what we have called "the paranormal." My first book, *Life After Life*, can no longer be, and should never have been, considered outside of the context of the material in *The Last Laugh*. To consider near-death experiences, or any other paranormal experience, outside of the new and larger context this book will create is to take the potatoes out of the oven before they are fully cooked. The results will be conclusions that are half-baked.

The fact that these are precisely the kinds of conclusions so many have come up with is, I think now, partly my fault. *Life After Life* was printed just as I wrote it, except that my publisher deleted the lengthy section at the end in which I explained in greater detail why near-death experiences can't be counted as scientific evidence of life after death.

The publisher worried that the appendix would go over the public's head. He said that no one would understand it and that, to a general reader, it would seem, in the final analysis, that I was taking back much of what I had said.

I didn't put up as much of a fight as it turns out I should have, and *Life After Life* was published with its last part missing. In my defense, I should say that, at that time, it never entered my mind that the book would become a major bestseller, that it would be of long-lasting interest to so many people the world over, that it would help set off a tidal wave of fascination with these unusual experiences, and, finally, that failure to insist on including there what I have included here would add to the stalemate effect.

Anyone who has monitored the dialogue on the nature of this phenomenon that has been going on now for two decades probably shares my impression that it has stagnated, with the same points being rehashed again and again. Even the cast of characters in the talk show confrontations on the subject has become stereotyped.

There is (a) the sympathetic physician or psychologist who has investigated the phenomenon and who is willing to allow that something unusual and important is going on; (b) the "scientific skeptic" who purports to explain it all away in terms of juddering neurons or oxygen deprivation or wishful thinking, and, on occasion, (c) the dour representative of the religious right who warns about demons and the torments of hell.

Deadlocked or not, the discussion will not go away. The fact that most of the "experts" have been getting nowhere in their attempts to come to some sort of conclusion (or even greater understanding) has done nothing to end the fascination of the public at large.

Interest in near-death experiences and the hereafter is now at a fever pitch, and scholars and clinicians will be discussing the subject for many years to come. In that climate, my stricken appendix will finally come home to roost. It is personally important to me that *Life After Life* be amended to accommodate the heretofore unreported information, as well as even later developments, not only so it will better reflect my original intentions and meanings, but also so that it will open up what are perhaps the first new areas for discussion on this topic in a quarter century—and offer new ways of exploring the topic itself.

Questioning the Basic Assumption

I'll begin with what for many of you may seem a new—and, considering the source, shocking—idea from me: there may be *no such thing as life after death.*

If I have unwittingly helped to create the impasse, maybe that statement will help break up the logjam. Logjams occur when everyone becomes "certain" about something—or as close to "certain" as nonevidentiary arguments can get. I'm afraid I have helped to make people feel "certain" about the existence of life after death because of my work in reporting near-death experiences. This is ironic, since *I* have never been certain.

What I am saying is that I have never equated—and I never meant to equate—my reporting of so-called "near death experiences" with a declaration on my part of the unquestioned existence of "life after death." The media did that. And my publishers did that, with the way they edited and marketed my book. I simply meant to report the experiences of people who were "near death." I never assumed myself to be reporting the experiences of people *after* death, nor have I ever reached the conclusion that because people were having certain kinds of experiences when they were near to death, an ongoing "life" after death had now been proven beyond question. The purpose of my first book, in fact, was to *raise* the question, not to *answer it.*

The purpose of this book, likewise, is not to *answer* this question, but to reopen it.

So now, here, let's look at what is really "so."

For decades now there has been a general presupposition that near-death experiences cannot safely and reliably be reproduced for study under conditions approximating a laboratory setting. This has left investigators with only retrospective first-person accounts upon which to base their assessments. Because persons offering these first-person accounts phrase their extraordinary personal narratives in terms of a life after death, we have automatically assumed that this means there is a life after death.

Yet, the visions of the dying offer no such positive proof, but merely provide data to be taken into the larger controversy.

And why have people offering their first-person accounts phrased their narratives in terms of a life after death? I submit that it is because this is the scenario with which they are most culturally familiar. That is, this is the only "logical" explanation their culture allows them to come up with—*il*logical as that explanation may be!

Movie and television writers call this the "back story." It is the background for what is now being experienced by the characters in their dramas. The back story provides a context, a rationalization, for their present-moment behaviors and conclusions.

The back story of our entire human culture has provided a backdrop against which the experiences some people have when they are "near death" are played out in their minds.

Thus, it is clear to me that, in order for us to consider those experiences as they have been interpreted as valid evidence of life after death, we must consider the context within which those first-person accounts have been offered.

This context includes our cultural stories about not only life after death, but stories surrounding *all* purportedly paranormal phenomena—stories that have been going around and around without letup since antiquity.

To help us understand any of these phenomena, so-called near-death experience among them, we have to understand why such stories have been going around for so long, why we are fascinated by them, and how we have been telling them.

It is to this exploration that the next section of this book will be devoted.

Changing the Ground Rules for This Discussion

The ground rules of this ancient controversy—that is, the ways in which we have allowed ourselves to explore and discuss the whole topic of the paranormal in the past—have themselves become part of the problem.

We can't allow this to go on. Genuine advances in the understanding of near-death experiences, as well as the public's hunger to know the truth at last about these topics that place such impact upon the meaning of life, require that the age-old wrangle about everything paranormal be reconceptualized by working out a new set of ground rules.

What we need is a new, and yet an old, way of thinking— one that will remain true to, while finally shedding the light of greater understanding upon, that most curious and alluring dimension of consciousness that we have called the paranormal.

So, that's where we're going to begin. We're going to take a look at the old way we've been discussing these issues up until now, and then we'll work into some new ways in which we can have those discussions from this point forward.

All of this will lead us on a journey that I think your mind will very much enjoy. And wouldn't it be interesting if, at the end of that journey, we decided that the "paranormal" was nothing of the sort, and that reported phenomena were nothing "other than" or "larger than" normal—but actually, quite normal after all?

I realize that this would tremendously upset the apple cart—an apple cart that I, myself, helped (however unwittingly) to set up—but I think it just might be time to do exactly that. Then we can see at last who, here, is going to have *the last laugh.*

2

PLAY AND THE PARANORMAL

As I've said, to really get anywhere in further discussions of near-death experiences, we must explore the larger subject of everything paranormal, and of everything that has been considered paranormal—which includes, it may surprise you to know, a great deal of what we have called "entertainment."

Then we must consider near-death experiences within the context of what that larger exploration reveals.

In this chapter, therefore, we are going to take what might seem, on the surface, to be a left turn. We are going to delve deeply into subjects other than near-death experiences, in order to lay the groundwork for understanding how we have collectively created a back story around them—a cultural backdrop, which, when understood, may help to explain how first-person accounts of near-death experiences have all come to sound so similar.

We are going to explore at length the connection between play and the paranormal, looking at everything from Ouija boards to dowsing to fortune-telling; from the "psychology of celebrity" to the phenomenon of "channeling."

We'll even look at madness as a function of the paranormal, and at the human penchant for making *everything* paranormal—from self-starvation to fire to claims of immunity from death. Finally, we'll explore the devices and tools of the paranormal that have played such a prominent role in writing our cultural story—from sounds to mirrors to wishing wells and mazes; from children's games to hobbies.

As I have warned, all of this may feel like a diversion of grand proportion, but I invite you to sit back and enjoy the ride. We'll come back to our discussion of near-death experiences and the question of life after death, I promise you. What I am attempting to do here is create a context within which that discussion can take place more fruitfully. You will see soon enough that this has not been a detour at all, but all part of the same journey.

The New "Rules of Engagement"

So now let's begin by looking at those ground rules I mentioned that need changing if we are to engage these old topics profitably. What have the ground rules been? Well, discussions of the paranormal have always given rise to a lively clash of opinions, appealing as they do to people of a broad range of temperaments. Interestingly, though, these clashes have nearly always fallen within certain parameters. The disagreements are nearly always the same, and it seems that nothing new has been said on this subject in years.

Until now.

What I have noticed is that most discussions and nearly all published materials devoted to the topic tend to reflect one of three distinct points of view, three contrasting schools of thought. These seem to be the most-often articulated positions; they are the "familiar, if inaccurate, perspectives" of which I spoke earlier. And the "ground rules" stipulate that discussion of the paranormal must fall into one of these categories.

The Parapsychologists' Point of View

The first category is the school of thought of "parapsychologists." these are people who perceive themselves to be scientists. There is a notion, widespread even among the skeptical, that the activity or field of study that investigates purportedly paranormal phenomena, happenings, or abilities is, or at least aspires to be, a subdiscipline of science.

Parapsychologically minded persons accept (at least in principle) that telepathy, psychokinesis, foreknowledge, life after death, and the like can be demonstrated by application of the scientific method.

The proponents of this point of view organize themselves in the form of various professional associations of parapsychology. Some have even sought, and obtained, membership in larger scientific societies, thereby "legitimizing" themselves.

The Skeptics' Point of View

The second category represents the school of thought of "skeptics"—those who are dubious to an extreme about supposedly paranormal happenings, experiences, or talents, which they feel surely can be explained away as fraud, hoax, wishful thinking, and error. They, too, have organized themselves into groups, such as the Committee for the Scientific Investigation of Claims of the Paranormal, a body that publishes a journal, the *Skeptical Inquirer.*

The Fundamentalists' Point of View

The third and final category is the school of thought of "fundamentalists." These are people who believe that all paranormal experiences are the work of the devil—and use Bible passages to prove it. The fundamentalists tell us that the being of light who greets many people during cardiac arrest, and the apparitions of the departed seen by the bereaved, are simply the tempter in disguise.

How These Categories Originated

Each of these three perspectives has its antecedents in very early times, and they are the fixtures of a continuing debate that goes back at least two millennia—and has still reached no conclusions.

Who can deny that little headway has been made? The whole controversy spins its wheels, endlessly turning on axes defined by those three major perspectives. It gives the illusion of motion, perhaps, but there is never a real forward component of progress. And there is a very good reason why not.

No One Watns *to Move Forward, No One* Wants *a Solution*

To date, the problems posed in the ongoing debate about the paranormal have not been solved because very few people *want* to solve them. Answers have been slow in coming because very few people *want* answers.

The problem with answers is that they eliminate the questions—and it's in the questions about the paranormal where we've found the most fun. It's what we *don't* know that fascinates us.

This is the reason that many controversies become irresolvable. Ironically, it is what is uncontested, not what is contested, that creates the logjam. It is the unspoken motivations held in common, or the unexamined assumptions in which all the parties acquiesce, at least tacitly, that allow the larger arguments to go on forever.

In the question of whether there is any reality to the paranormal, the proponents of the three schools of thought share a common unspoken motivation to keep the debate going, and that motivation is, ironically, their own fascinated absorption with the paranormal. They all want to keep looking at it. To resolve anything would be to end the discussion—and this is a discussion no one wants to see concluded.

The reasons may be obvious in the case of the professional parapsychologists—the category one people—who, after all, have made the paranormal their life's work. But the organized pseudo-skeptics—the category two folks, also relish the subject. They write papers, attend meetings, carry out field investigations, and openly admit they have the bug. Even the zealous fundamentalists from category three seem to get a visible buzz from unveiling a demon in every dream, Satan at every seance, and the Antichrist behind every apparition.

There's a twitter of excitement in all of this for everyone, and these three are far from the only groups held in a trance by the paranormal's irresistible charm. The truth is, most of us are drawn to these things. Like the flames of a fire, the invitations of the paranormal dance tantalizingly before our collective consciousness, and we are transfixed by the mystery, awed by the splendor, and, in our fearful moments, afraid of the power of it all. Even those who say they fear the paranormal are at some level fascinated by it.

Why We Are So Transfixed

What is the basis of this appeal? Why is it, and how is it, that so many of us have come to be enraptured and entranced by the paranormal, and get caught up in its spell? What, precisely, is the nature of the human concern with the paranormal? We cannot answer any question of the validity of near-death experiences as evidence of life after death without answering these questions first, for when we understand the answer to these questions, we begin to understand the paranormal itself. We begin to see that broad aspect of human endeavor to which the paranormal is most naturally related. We begin to see connections—connections that allow us to start to make some sense of it all. We begin to put it all together in ways we never have before. And the puzzle of the paranormal begins to solve itself. The mystery starts to unravel. And we can then create a new context within which to consider the primary topic of our exploration: near-death experiences and life after death.

The Paranormal as "Entertainment"

And now, here is my hypothesis. You may find it difficult to embrace at first, but wait. Give me a little time. I think I can convince you. And if I can't, I'll at least have opened up a new area of discussion. So here goes.

I believe we are entranced by the paranormal because we are entertained by it.

Now this may seem obvious to you, yet I believe that this link between entertainment and the paranormal is often overlooked, and that the implications of this link may not be so obvious. Certainly, they have rarely been previously explored.

I have become increasingly aware of how entertainment, humor, play, and the paranormal are, in a curious way, intimately enmeshed. And I argue that it is this enmeshment that has created the context within which we have always considered the paranormal, and now consider near-death experiences. I believe that it is what I call this entertainment factor that has created our back story around life after death. Now, mind you, this does not automatically eliminate the validity of life after death claims. It is just possible, after all, that, by whatever means, we have stumbled upon a great truth. It is nevertheless important—indeed, more important, should this be so—that we know all we can know about that which caused us to stumble.

Looking at What's Held in Common

Each of these—entertainment, humor, play—share a distinguishing and common feature with what we call the paranormal. Each is defined in terms of a contrast with what is deemed ordinary reality, as is the paranormal. Each challenges and expands our conceptions of reality, of the limits of the mind, and of the nature of consciousness, as does the paranormal.

Let's look at these ideas a bit.

For the great majority of those who pursue it, the study of the paranormal is, like entertainment and play, a leisure time activity. Legions of enthusiasts from every walk of life belong to clubs or other organizations devoted to the paranormal.

The various techniques for discovering hidden knowledge constitute a major branch of the paranormal, and in their natural setting several forms of "divination" are parlor games. Ouija boards, table tapping, tarot, and runes are examples.

Tarot employs playing cards, not unlike Old Maid or poker, while runes uses little game pieces, not unlike Monopoly or Scrabble. Ouija boards are sold in toy stores. The owner of the firm that manufactures the board and the gadget that comes with it is reported to have been astounded when people took it seriously. He went to his grave protesting that it was just a game.

Dowsing for water with divining rods has gamelike aspects, too—except when done by people wandering in the desert, or preparing to spend thousands of dollars digging a well on their property.

Fortune-tellers' parlors are found at amusement parks, beachside boardwalks, and grammar school festivals. Many newspapers print astrology columns alongside the comic strips. (Serious publications such as the *New York Times* exclude both from their pages.)

Even the Law Sees the Connection

Our common law is a storehouse of practical wisdom—the accumulated, consensual rulings of many centuries' seasoned jurists. Practically speaking, the legal tradition is a handy guide to what experienced jurists-deciders have decided, often under perplexing circumstances, about a widely diverse calendar of hotly contested and tricky issues. In effect, the law reflects the opinion of the practical person of wisdom and experience. And what does common law have to say about the paranormal?

You guessed it. On more than a few occasions the law has ruled that the paranormal is *entertainment*. In some jurisdictions fortune-tellers, astrologers, and psychics are actually classified, for the purpose of licensure, as *recreation workers.*

The haunted house is a fixture of the amusement park, and the paranormal is even celebrated as a holiday—Halloween. What are known as "psychic fairs" are common weekend diversions throughout the country.

The past-life regressions that are now so much in vogue immediately bring the craft of the historical novelist to mind, making one wonder what connections could be uncovered between that mystifying form of paranormal adventure and a popular, entertaining variety of leisure-time fiction.

Actors portray persons of long ago on stage and in movies. Inner journeys back to previous lives seem a lot like that, except that the drama is enacted within the mind, with the functions of playwright, producer, director, actor, audience, and set designer being variably shared between paranormal time traveler and past-life regressionist.

Ghost stories, accounts of apparently telepathic communications between friends, and tales about premonitions are among the basic subject matter of the study of the paranormal. In this respect, it overlaps with the study of folklore, and one self-evident purpose of folklore is to amuse and to entertain.

Paranormal happenings lend themselves quite naturally to presentation in dramatic form, and it is often observed that the histrionic traits of personality that make for good actors and actresses can make, also, for good psychics.

Given the possibility of fraud, most investigators of the paranormal accept that claims as to the occurrence of certain allegedly paranormal phenomena are often best tested by stage magicians expert in the creation of illusion and deception. Magicians are entertainers.

Celebrities and the Paranormal: The Connection Broadens

The connection between the paranormal and entertainment becomes more and more obvious the closer one explores it. The status of famous entertainers in modern society is exactly that held in the ancient world by certain supernatural entities—spirits and the like. Celebrated entertainers—Rudolph Valentino, James Dean, Marilyn Monroe, and Elvis Presley, for example—have been made the objects of cult-like adoration. The most popular movie actors and actresses are even called "stars," a perhaps-not-too coincidental celestial metaphor that signifies selfhood set above, in a heavenly realm. This is a stratagem of language that hearkens back to an age of astrology.

The phenomenon of dwelling on the lives of celebrities probably relates to the fact that modern humans spend a sizable proportion of their waking hours attending to images and information promulgated by the media. As people whose identities society has appropriated for its symbolic purposes, celebrities, because they are capable of appearing "in person," constitute a link between the world revealed through the media and the world of everyday life. Hence, celebrities are intermediary beings, serving to reassure us, on a subconscious level, of the "reality" of the electronic dimension in which we seem somehow also to live.

Because celebrities can pass back and forth between alternate realities, the concept of celebrity resonates with the concept of the paranormal. Like the paranormal, celebrity gets a lot of mileage out of death. Given their unique station within the social order, super celebrities are not entitled to an ordinary departure. Tens of millions of ordinary folks may carry on fantasized relationships with a single such semi-imaginary personage. When superstars die, the artificiality of fan-celebrity relationships can beget astonishing perturbations of the grieving process.

The after-Elvis phenomenon that followed the Great Gyrator's death in 1977 is the most familiar recent example. After the tragedy of Elvis's death, rumors ran riot among uncomprehending fans. Those who were inclined to do so believed that Elvis had conspired to simulate his own death, staging a mock funeral complete with convincingly real, weeping family mourners. The centerpiece of that well-publicized event was rumored to have been only an effigial coffin insert. The believers entertained the notion that their hero had taken flight to Hawaii, the land far to the west, there to live apart from a crushing overload of popularity.

A wave of Elvis sightings swept the country. Many of his fans experienced what they felt was psychic contact with Elvis from the beyond. As of this writing, almost twenty years later, a measurable percentage of the American population still say they believe that the singer may not be dead, but is in hiding.

Mixing Our Psychologies Produces Our Realities

The psychology of celebrity has been mingling with the psychology of the paranormal for a long time. And, lest you think that Elvis was the first popular musician to acquire a reputation for putting in after-death appearances paranormally, let me offer evidence to the contrary.

The ancient Greek historian Herodotus (490–425 B.C.) recorded the escapades of an entertainer who also reputedly juggled his musical fame to create a spurious death and to arrange for subsequent spectral reappearances:

> More information about [a remote] part of the world is to be found in a poem by Aristeas . . . a native of Marmora island. He tells us that "inspired by [Apollo]" he journeyed to the country of the Issedones, and that beyond the Issedones live the one-eyed Arimaspians, and beyond them the griffins which guard the gold, and beyond the griffins the Hyperboreans, whose land comes down to the sea. . . .
>
> Here is a story I heard about him in Marmora and Cyzicus. He belonged to one of the first families in his home town, and one day, upon entering a fuller's shop, he fell down dead. The fuller closed his shop and hurried out to inform his relatives of what had occurred, but no sooner had the news of Aristeas' death got

about, than a person from Cyzicus, who had just arrived from the town of Artaca, contradicted the rumor and declared that he had met him going towards Cyzicus and had talked to him. He was absolutely certain of this and would take no denial. Meanwhile, Aristeas' relatives were on their way to the shop with what was necessary for the funeral, intending to take the body away; they opened the door, and the room was empty—Aristeas was not there, either dead or alive. Seven years later he reappeared in Marmora, wrote the poem we now call the "Tale of the Arimaspians," and again vanished. I will add something which I know happened to the people of Metapontum in Italy two hundred and forty years (as I found by computation) after the second disappearance of Aristeas.

There the story goes that Aristeas appeared and told them to erect an altar to Apollo, with a statue beside it bearing the name of Aristeas of Marmora; then, after explaining that they were the only people in Italy whom Apollo had visited, and that he himself on the occasion of his visit had accompanied the god in the form of a raven, he vanished. The Metapontines sent to Delphi to ask the oracle what the apparition signified, and were advised that they had better do what it recommended. This advice they took, with the result that in the market-square of the town a statue inscribed with the name of Aristeas stands today by the side of the image of Apollo, surrounded by myrtle bushes.

Aristeas was seen to die, then he was reported alive, and then he—or his body—was discovered to be missing. Was it a death, or a mysterious disappearance? Or both? Since the fuller had locked the door to his shop upon leaving, there was a Houdini element of magical escape to it as well.

By his departure, Aristeas created a crazy-quilt of perplexities and ambiguities. Then, while in some sort of trance or other altered state of consciousness, he set out on an extended journey among the weird inhabitants of lands beyond the boundaries of the known world, a touristy nirvana he recounted in a poetic travelogue.

Seven years later, when he reappeared, he presumably would have been relegated to the curious social status of a *deuteropotmos,* or twice-fated one. This social category included persons who had gone too far into the near beyond to be readmitted to the land of the living. A person who had been assumed dead abroad, for example, but who subsequently returned, would be declared a *deuteropotmos.* Such people might be forbidden to mix with others, and they were excluded from sanctuaries.

Aristeas's performance was brilliantly contrived, even if only preconsciously or subconsciously so. He skillfully deployed techniques at the nebulous interface between drama and histrionics. By vanishing from Marmora a second time, he created a legend for himself that helped precipitate his apparitional reappearance. While alive, he set in motion a process that two hundred and forty years later confirmed and cemented his reputation as a person who could shuttle back and forth across the Great Divide.

The Point of All This

The luminaries of the entertainment business today continue to play a major role in influencing public attitudes toward paranormal phenomena. Fans of the paranormal are quick to make celebrities, especially famous performers, the anointed authorities on the subject.

In the 1980s a talented, articulate, comic actress opened up publicly about her own supernatural experiences, and promptly became a respected spokesperson for the paranormal. Her name lent added impulse to a mounting wave of public interest in such phenomena. The public went "out on a limb" to accept that her experiences were real, but it wanted them to be—and that is precisely my point.

This is the implication—the fallout, if you will—of the connection between entertainment and the paranormal of which I said there has been very little serious exploration.

Could it be that there is a cause-and-effect relationship here? Are we creating that which we call the paranormal out of our desire to do so?

The "scientific skeptics" have a good laugh, and enjoy poking fun, at how celebrities are given "expert" status, and at the feeble logic of all advocates of the paranormal. Then, oddly, these same "debunkers" turn right around and adduce countervailing celebrity endorsements to validate their own cause. The pseudo-skeptics' organization lists a famous television musician and comedian on their honor roll of celebrity dubitantes. Thus, it would appear that even the pseudo-skeptics are clear about how powerful a factor celebrity worship is in the world of the paranormal.

It is so powerful, in fact, that it has a "reverse-English effect" on serious students and researchers of the paranormal, who themselves become celebrities by simple virtue of their association with the subject in the public's eye. (I can ruefully attest to that.)

Our Exploration of the Back Story Expands

No forthright and thoroughgoing examination of the paranormal and life after death can forego analyzing how the psychology of celebrity helps shape the public's perceptions of both, and of who the experts on the supernatural are. This is all part of our back story.

This is a pressing issue, because the paranormal is one of the more common topics discussed on talk shows. "Experts" on the subject are probably seen by the public on talk shows more often than in any other type of forum. They are having a lot to say on the subject, and the public is believing what they are saying.

I am not exaggerating when I say that admiring believers treat the renowned "experts" who are proponents of the paranormal like celebrities, like famous entertainers, rather than in the way eminent experts in more conventional fields of science and scholarship are treated. The fans even ask us for our autographs!

But those same nice folks respond to prominent experts who are skeptical of the paranormal as they would be to sinister stage villains, figuratively booing and hissing them, as many a professional debunker could testify. We wise, proparanormal "experts" understand how the skeptics must feel, though, because fundamentalist authorities on the occult figuratively boo and hiss us, taking us to task for being "agents of Satan," and casting us as archvillains in demonic, horrific melodramas taking place deep within their minds.

Although we may have originally been labeled an "expert in the field" because of our advanced degrees in subjects such as medicine or psychology, in fact, many of us constantly travel from city to city and hotel to hotel to make public appearances, thus behaving just like entertainers, and very much unlike conventional medical doctors or psychologists. We act like the celebrities the public has made us.

The Paranormal/Entertainment Connection: Is It Exaggerated?

Have I overstated the point about the paranormal and entertainment, and how the two have always been almost as one to many people for a very long time? I don't think so. There are numerous persons whose lives could as readily be included in the history of the paranormal as in that of entertainment. One of my favorites is the wonderful Lulu Hurst, immortalized as the Georgia Magnet.

In the summer of 1883, when Lulu was fifteen, what could easily be classified as poltergeist disturbances began in her family's home. Dishes began to fly around and break, objects dropped to the floor for no discernible reason, and strange sounds were heard. Lulu referred to her power as the great unknown, and within a short time she was mystifying audiences in Atlanta, Chicago, and New York.

She appeared to be able effortlessly to push several strong people around the stage at once, despite their best efforts to resist, as though they had been paralyzed by some magical power. It was an astonishing demonstration, but after only a couple of years on the circuit, she confessed that it was all done by trickery. Claiming that she was alarmed by the superstitious incredulity of her audiences, she then retired. Today, though, she is mentioned in some books about the paranormal as though she had strange (and real) powers.

Her life could make an interesting case for the argument favoring a very real paranormal/entertainment connection. What initially appeared to be a poltergeist occurrence quickly evolved into a stage show—and what was finally acknowledged to be a stage show devolved back into the paranormal years later.

Many great entertainers could have easily passed off their talents as supernatural wonders—Harry Houdini, for example. This "reverse-English" effect gives rise to one of the most frequently heard accusations made about what might actually be a demonstration of something genuinely paranormal: that it is, in fact, "just" entertainment. The controversy about Uri Geller offers a good contemporary example.

Our confusion about all of this thus produces a transposition: Houdini—acknowledged, after all, as nothing more than a great magician—is labeled supernatural, and Geller—whom many investigators believe to possess genuine psychic power— is called entertaining. Our penchant for doing this transposing and intermixing is, as I have said, not recent, but ancient.

When it emerged from the mists of prehistory, the entertainment industry already was conjoined with the paranormal.

Even in Ancient Greece

Entertainment always has depended not solely on performers, but also on creative writers. There must be a steady supply of new material to keep an easily bored public amused. From very early times, poets and dramatists surmised that their gifts sprang from an independent spiritual source. So did the public.

The ancient Greeks personified creative inspiration as the Muses, feminine spirits who were consulted at their special places, the *museions*. Hence, an early mixing of entertainment and the paranormal.

Sometimes, someone receives the gift of creativity in the course of a paranormal experience. The ancient Greek poet Hesiod's works are among the oldest surviving written relics of the Western literary tradition. Hesiod took up the music business because the Muses instructed him to do so. Hesiod caught sight of the Muses dancing around a spring one day as he grazed his sheep on Mount Helicon. "We know how to make up fancy lies, it is true, but we also can tell the truth, when we've a mind to," the Muses sang to the shepherd. After his vision, Hesiod devoted his life to making poetry and song.

In a work that some regard as the earliest history of England, *The Venerable Bede* (673–735 A.D.) recorded the story of a man who was transformed overnight into a great poet and songwriter by a powerful supernatural visitation. The story's hero, Caedmon, was a shy person and at dinners, when by custom each person sang for the whole party, Caedmon always found some excuse to hurry away in embarrassment.

One evening, after just such an episode, he slept in the cattle byre, because it was his night to stay on guard there. As he slept, he had a vision in which someone standing beside him in the darkness said, "Sing to me, Caedmon." Caedmon replied that he could not sing; that had been why he had left the feast early. The figure persisted, "Sing to me, anyway. Sing about the beginnings of the world."

Caedmon burst forth in melodious songs; they were verses he had never heard before. When he awoke the next morning, he still had his new and miraculous talent. Caedmon spent the rest of his days making music with his preternatural gift, and his verses enjoyed a holy reputation far and wide.

In fact, it is a fairly common experience among artists and writers to have an uncanny feeling that their works emanate from sources outside of themselves.

What Is the Source? That's the Ancient Question

Goethe maintained that only one of the works attributed to him (namely, the second part of *Faust*) was actually his own composition. He implied that he channeled the rest of them from some spiritual source beyond himself.

According to Richard Bach, *Jonathan Livingston Seagull* was dictated to him by a disembodied voice. And the most recent (and perhaps the most striking) example of this is a trilogy of books called *Conversations with God,* which has sold millions of copies, remained on best-seller lists well over a hundred weeks, and has been translated into twenty-four languages around the world. Its author, Neale Donald Walsch, says he has received his material directly from God.

Many writers claim to have had a strange feeling of being "led" to an essential reference, or given a singular inspiration, at a critical juncture of a project. So the Greeks' idea of Muses may seem a better intuitive fit to some of the anomalies of the inner lives of persons engaged in creative work.

The modern reformulation of the concept attempts to move the locus of control of the creative process to within the writer or artist, but in the good old days a work of genius was one over which the artist or writer was assumed to have had little or no control.

By contrast, the contemporary definition of genius in terms of high I.Q. seems to have no heart. The outcome of this has been that an entire, historically important category of eerily baffling, but fairly common, experiences familiar to many creatively gifted people remains unappreciated by mainline psychology. In other words, because mainline psychology accepts the contemporary, somewhat flat definition of genius, the genuine source of the inspirations received by creative types is never rigorously explored. Thus, the possibility of a connection between the entertainment provided by these gifted artists and writers and paranormal phenomena continues to be ignored—a point I made earlier. And so long as it is ignored, there will be confusion about what we call the paranormal—and, by extension, about life after death.

That confusion is, of course, what this book hopes to end.

And Now, Mix in "Madness"

The confusion between what is paranormal and what is entertainment has grown even more complex as society placed some behaviors found in both categories into a third category altogether: madness, or mental illness.

Certain conditions originally regarded as paranormal went through a stage of being exploited for entertainment purposes on their way to being reconceptualized in this manner. For instance, a complex of behaviors and thought patterns related to food—specifically, obsessional thinking and talking about food, chronic self-starvation, and perfectionism and hyperactivity, especially in adolescent women—was once known as anorexia mirabilis and was regarded as a supernatural phenomenon.

In the fourteenth century, Catherine of Siena was the most famous of a number of women who were able to gain a reputation for holiness by incorporating this complex into their religious preoccupations. Catherine deprived herself of food for extended periods and yet remained very energetic. She was eventually canonized as a saint. Today, she would be diagnosed as having anorexia nervosa, a psychiatric illness—as are all young women who starve themselves in the same manner.

During the latter part of the nineteenth century, a similar or identical complex was commercialized by the so-called Fasting Girls of Britain and America. They drew large crowds by publicly starving themselves. A carnival atmosphere surrounded the homes where these girls confined themselves to bed. Spectators, many bearing gifts, arrived from far and wide. The mother of one of the young women even bedizened her daughter, shaman-like, in a costume of ribbons and a fancy headdress.

The Victorians enjoyed the festive entertainment, but they weren't quite sure whether the Fasting Girls represented something supernatural or not. So, the strange and trendy outbreak of noneating fueled a hot debate between parapsychologically minded supporters and crusty, scientific debunkers. "Funda-Christian" preachers warned of the influence of demons. And so, our three categories of debaters each got in their licks.

A parallel development took place in attitudes toward congenital anomalies and malformations. In the ancient world, Siamese twins and persons born with too many or too few limbs, as well as others with obvious developmental variations, were regarded as omens—supernatural signs of bad things to come.

The Victorian era saw the development of dehumanizing "freak shows," in which deformed people were displayed for the amusement of others. Today, developmental anomalies have been reclassified as medical conditions. We look to scientists for explanation, and to physicians for treatment.

In the medieval period, it was widely believed that some people could transform themselves into wolves, or could return from the dead to feed on the blood of their hapless victims. The literary imagination eventually tamed these beliefs into a popular genre of entertainment, with werewolf and vampire books and movies abounding. Today, psychiatrists regard lycanthropy, other zooanthropic delusions, and vampirism as rare, but indubitably real, psychopathological entities.

Originally, madness was thought to be a paranormal phenomenon. Ancient medical authorities assigned supernatural causes to mental disturbance. Medieval doctors thought demons were to blame.

From there, madness came up through the ranks into entertainment. In the eighteenth century, Bedlam was one of London's principal sightseeing attractions. Beleaguered administrators defrayed the cost of keeping up the madhouse by opening its doors to the gawking public. Sightseers paid an admission price to poke fun and laugh at deranged inmates.

Twentieth century physicians diagnosed psychosis on the medical model. Psychiatry has made madness a matter of biochemistry.

None of this is to imply that there is an ineluctable progression toward scientific enlightenment that will inevitably dispel primeval superstition. The picture is more complex than that. For example, sometimes people with anorexia nervosa say that the interesting altered states of awareness brought about by self-starvation are part of their motivation for maintaining the behavior. Indeed, fasting has historically been a popular means for attaining mystical states.

The development, over time, of the public perception of anorexia, genetic or developmental aberrations, werewolves and vampires, and psychosis, does suggest, though, that entertainment can be a way station, an intermediate form with deep-seated connections both with the supernatural and with science. It may even be the trigger that allows some of these experiences to be produced.

The Human Penchant for Making Everything Paranormal

Even attitudes toward natural phenomena can shift when the mind is entertained.

Early humans regarded fire with profound awe and veneration; they even worshiped it. Bonfires originally were built for purposes of paranormality. The bodies of sacrificial animals were set afire so that augurs might divine the future by attending to the snapping, crackling, and popping of the burning carcasses. It turns out that "bone-fires" were literally that. The "Funda-Christians" once fueled their bone-fires with those they labeled witches and heretics. Nowadays, bonfires are set in celebration, and dictionaries note that they are for entertainment.

In the nineteenth century, tricksters such as Ivan Chabert and Signora Josephine Giardelli (the Fireproof Woman) seriously presented themselves as being incombustible. During stage shows, they demonstrated such talents as swallowing boiling oil and putting molten lead in their mouths, and many spectators accepted that the performers had preternatural powers.

Today, we are all familiar with entertainers who swallow fire, and we feel no need to assume anything paranormal is taking place. In modern America, fire gazing is an innocuous childhood pastime, but shamans in Australia once divined the future by discerning figures in funeral fires.

The concept of paranormal fire is still with us in the form of tales of spontaneous human combustion. And walking on fire is still included among the paranormal feats (or feets!) attributed to holy men.

On what grounds, though, would a fire swallower be classified as an entertainer, but a fire walker as a miracle worker? Would a person swallowing fire while walking over hot coals be considered an entertainer or a prophet? Fire—a natural phenomenon—fuses entertainment with the paranormal into an undifferentiated whole.

Then, Too, There's the "I Don't Die" Game.

Playing with your food and playing with fire were not the only activities connecting the paranormal with entertainment.

In centuries gone by, there were those who claimed to enjoy a paranormal immunity from death, and who were believed to be of extreme age.

Artephius, born early in the twelfth century, wrote a famous book on the art of prolonging human life, in which he claimed to be an expert on the subject by virtue of being one thousand and twenty-five years old. He had many believing admirers who whiled away their time by constructing logical proofs that he was as old as he claimed.

Artephius had an excellent memory and had developed an expert's command of the facts of history. He applied his rich imagination to this wealth of historical information to weave a tapestry of colorful reminiscences about an impressive repertoire of famous historical figures. He had a great talent for appearing just as though he were remembering the exact details of their appearance, mannerisms, and personality.

Half a millennium later, Count de Saint Germain became an important figure in the court of King Louis XV of France by claiming to have discovered an elixir with which he could make anyone live for centuries. He allowed it to be generally believed that he was over two thousand years old. Like his predecessor Artephius, he had read history extensively and had a wonderful memory. He was never at a loss when he was interrogated as to the details of the lives of great persons of the past. He spoke of his conversations with historical figures long dead with such apparent sincerity and in such abundant detail (including particulars of their appearance and dress and even the weather at the time, and the furniture in the room) that many who came to scoff went away convinced. A well-known countess even came to believe that she had known him fifty years earlier and testified that he hadn't aged a bit since then.

Count de Saint Germain dressed in a magnificent style, made a display of costly jewels, and from time to time bestowed expensive gifts on members of the court. The king respected him greatly, often conversed with him in private for hours, and would not let others speak disparagingly of him.

No one ever discovered what the count's real name was, and incredible beliefs sprang up as to his true identity. Many debunkers alleged he was a spy employed by England, but no evidence supporting the charge ever came to light.

He managed to surround himself with a dramatic aura of mystery by not letting anyone know how he lived and by refraining from unequivocally contradicting the rumors about his great age. Among more critical persons, he denied he was really the age he was popularly reputed to be, but he did so in a manner that, as if inadvertently, actually reinforced that very impression. He was often accompanied by a servant, who claimed to have been with him for five hundred years and corroborated the count's recollections.

The kind of knowledge and skills that Artephius and Count de Saint Germain required in order to make the impression they did are, in important respects, the same as those of the entertainers who, today, are noted for their special talent for evoking on stage a solo appearance in person by a noted historical personage. Mark Twain, Harry Truman, and Elvis Presley have all been portrayed in this way by various performers.

In the twentieth century, birth records and scientific techniques of fingerprint and DNA identification make it much more difficult to pull off a bogus claim of being wondrously immune to death. Still, the concept has undeniable emotional and entertainment appeal. It survives today as the premise of "The Two Thousand Year Old Man," an hilarious work of comic artistry by Mel Brooks and Carl Reiner.

Wondrous immunities to flames, to starvation, to death, and to other slings and arrows of outrageous fortune make up a distinct subclass of purportedly paranormal phenomena or abilities. But holy folks have to share the spotlight with entertainers on the stage of supernatural imperviousness, because many of those with wondrous immunities love to go into show business.

Examples of some "latter-day saints" of this variety could be the dozens of people who do not claim immunity from death, but who are nonetheless reputed (or imagined by the public) to have grander spiritual knowledge, higher wisdom, or deeper understanding of eternal truths, and who literally "take to the stage" at so-called "whole life" expositions, body-mind-soul conferences, and various other traveling shows from coast to coast. Anyone who doubts that the paranormal has continued to this very day to be entertainment has never seen a presentation by Dannion Brinkley or Neale Donald Walsch— the first of whom purports to have come back from the dead, the second of whom says he's talked directly to God. Both are showmen of the first rank, and indeed, both make the points they seek to make impressively and effectively for precisely this reason. And they are not the only ones on "the circuit" these days who fall into that category.

But the paranormal immunities in particular, being a transitional form, have a lot to divulge about the relationship between the paranormal and entertainment, and about what some of the factors are that make a thing one or the other. Thinking about wondrous immunities also uncovers some secret traps the paranormal sets to ensnare all but the most careful and uncompromising thoughts before they can discover its strange inner nature.

Lying down on his bare back on a bed that bristles with real, sharply pointed, metal nails, and then reclining there comfortably and unbleeding for quite a while, smiling and chatting with disciples or passersby, has for a long time been enough for a man to do to become known as a perisacred person with paranormal powers. The image of a prophet supine on his spiky mattress is an occasional icon of parahuman holiness.

Where Does Holiness End and Show Business Begin? A Closer Look at "Wondrous Immunities"

In 1995 a showman took to the circuit displaying that very talent, but for the express purpose of entertaining. Typically, he hauls his heavy, scary mat onto the stage for spectators' close inspections, and they attest to its tough-as-nails reality. Then he plops himself down harmlessly, bare back to sharp nails, and reposes there unpunctured, not flinching, not pleading for medical assistance, not talking in a screechy tone of voice, not receiving an IV drip of morphine, not passing out or lapsing into coma. By the merest act of resting there without screaming away his last few preethereal moments, he alights in onlookers a wonder that has for a long time been felt as something paranormal.

He is decked out in a brightly colored costume that is an amalgamation of those of all the turbaned fakirs of the paranormal's childhood imagination. The symbolism of his outfit is the only vestment of paranormal meaning left in this man or in his act, however.

After a while, the man takes his audience along on an escalation of human impossibility. He lies on his bed of nails, clasping a concrete block to his chest, and rests there unblinking, as a young man selected from the third row of seats swings a sledge hammer down, smashing the concrete into several hefty chunks.

Somewhere in there, all this got to be a bit much for the paranormal, and it took its leave in favor of entertainment. The sledge hammer and concrete are too much paranormal for anyone's common sense to accept, or for belief to be sustained. At some point along a progression (and specifying exactly where may be difficult), what originally was a paranormal effect gives way to an entertaining one.

Of course, someone could restore the paranormal to the bed of nails act. It could be "reparanormalized" by adding a weird tint of dim lighting, soft, eerie music, and/or a little preliminary "guru-talk" about getting in touch with just the right supernatural vibrations, or creating the appropriate energies, or some such thing.

The general rule is: if it is too much like "just fun," then the paranormal effect is gone. The paranormal wouldn't want to have anything to do with a man strolling barefoot across blazing hot coals while toasting marshmallows on the tip of a pointed stick. (Take away the marshmallows and you have a chance.)

The point: the paranormal can "lose it" when things gets too close to comedy.

Physicists give compelling proof of their own ideas, to the contrary of the paranormal's, about the dangerousness of ordinary humans lying down on a bed of nails. Their demonstration is so complete that, after seeing it, even many sane individuals would leap at the chance to perform that once-supernatural wonder (under the close, expert supervision of a hallowed person or stage performer, of course).

The same is true of fire walking. These days one doesn't have to be a miracle-worker to be a fire walker. So-called "fire walks" are now a staple at many New Age "festivals" and "personal growth retreats," where participants step right out of the audience and right onto a bed of glowing coals, scampering across without apparent ill-effect, to their own astonishment.

This is, in fact, the point of those fire walks. Their promoters and sponsors will tell you straight out that they are seeking to show participants that there is nothing abnormal at all about human beings doing "superhuman" things, and indeed, once people have done a fire walk, many do feel greater self-confidence, display a deeper awareness of their own innate (and perfectly normal) abilities, and produce larger results in their lives.

And so, the paranormal is left standing speechless about those old bed-of-nails and fire-walk tricks. But since this wonder now is coming so fresh from a long run of reputed paranormality, it affords an excellent opportunity to glimpse pure entertainment-in-the-making derived from the recently paranormal.

Could There Be More than Just a "Connection"?

There is this idea that keeps cropping up. Maybe there is no difference between that which is entertaining and that which is paranormal. Maybe the two really *are* one.

Maybe what we are talking about here is more than just a "connection." Maybe there is nothing to "connect," because there is only one experience, only one effect.

Both the entertainment quotient of "wondrous immunity," for instance, and its quotient of paranormality, derive from seeing someone accomplish something an average bystander would strongly suppose humanly impossible, and performing that seeming impossibility safely and with apparent ease. So here it can be seen how closely the effect of being entertaining can coincide with the effect of being paranormal.

Wondrous immunities strike people as paranormal because they seem to be so far beyond what appears humanly possible in the way of fleshly imperviousness. The felt wonder of the spectators comes from the shifting of their own inner limits of human possibility. Taking in such a sight can cause one's inner boundaries to be redrawn, to now encompass something that was previously felt to be outside the range human of possibility—and that experience of possibilities-expansion is very entertaining to the human mind.

Interestingly, it often makes no difference whether a person is participating in the event as a spectator or as a paranormal immunist. Seeing someone else enact a wondrous feat of that type can sometimes be just as effective as performing it oneself (for the first time, or the first few times). Of course, if simply watching is powerful, *doing* what is being watched can be life-changing! What a dazzling and ebullient realization it must be to not only *realize* that one can walk on hot glowing coals unshod and unscathed, lie down on sharp nails unharmed, or starve oneself beyond what is thought of as the nether edge of oblivion, but to *experience* it. The thrill that accompanies the advent of such firsthand knowledge is a major part of the enduring appeal of the wondrous immunities.

Lately, the paranormal has been taking an army of fun-loving Americans along with it on one of these adventures. Today, there are more American fire walkers, beginning and experienced, than all the firefighters can squirt their extinguishers at.

Thinking about the wondrous immunities also reveals that the paranormal can be arbitrary and two-timing. It certainly acts erratically and capriciously when it passes out its seeming exemptions from baseline bodily humanity. So, a holy man in training must read his manual carefully and not get the instructions mixed up by lying down on his bare back on a bed of hot coals, or walking barefoot across a bed of sharp, uppity nails.

And the paranormal doesn't permit a squeamish beginner to build up confidence by practicing lying down on just one or two nails at first.

The paranormal immunities echo with all the force of some of our parents' scariest, most insistent early admonitions: eat your vegetables; think of the starving children elsewhere; beware of fire and of sharp, pointy objects; and whatever you do, don't die or get killed. From that point of view, it is helpful to examine the case of a wonderful performer named Captain Dynamite—another performer who would have us believe that he can cheat death.

"Death-Cheaters" Continue to Bridge the Gap between the Paranormal and Entertainment

The case of Captain Dynamite is a good one for illustrating how wondrous immunity abuts on entertainment pure and simple. This astounding dynamite-resister's act trails off into the domain of professional daredevils; and there the paranormal is again, this time in the very name *daredevil*, probably bestowed upon the trade by a grumpy fundamentalist of days gone by.

Thickly clad in motorcyclist's suit and helmet, the man who calls himself Captain Dynamite presents himself in a sports arena, an area about the size of a football field or baseball diamond being required for the captain's particular near-death enactment. Then he quickly wows the crowd by standing up to the mighty dynamite blast he deliberately sets off only a matter of feet in front of himself. A couple of minutes later he rolls deftly out of a tight wooden box that has just been blown apart by another exploding stick of dynamite, then springs to his feet to receive the audience's loud applause—if he can hear it.

All that Captain Dynamite does before his watchers' very eyes certainly seems to transcend what the average person might imagine to be humanly possible. His act goes beyond what common sense seems to know about human survivability. Yet, here there is no hint of the paranormal in the act itself. The good captain does not even give a bow to it in fond remembrance.

Perhaps this is because he knows that parents don't have to train their young children to remain ever-wary of dynamite blasts specifically, at least over most of the planet thus far. Perhaps dynamite explosions aren't sufficiently primeval in their fearful prohibitiveness to be staged as a paranormal immunity.

Anyway, it probably would be impossible to get any paranormal play out of surviving a dynamite blast wearing substantial protective covering. Dark purple loincloth and sandals would be more what the paranormal would require, but it probably wouldn't even let that in.

Saint Dynamite would be a hard sell, paranormally.

Using Sounds to Make the Connection

The art of producing sounds in such a way that they seem to originate from a source other than the speaker has become a recognized form of pop entertainment. The bond between the performer and his or her puppet figure remains a subject for paranormal speculation, however.

From time to time, persons attending shamanic or mediumistic ceremonies have reported hearing seemingly disembodied voices having no apparent source. Chukchee shamans, for example, were said to have separate voices, and participants at their sessions heard spirit vocalizations rising from the corners of the room.

Authorities who are believers may interpret phantom speech as being of supernatural causation. Some pseudo-skeptical investigators, on the other hand, have attempted to explain these observations in terms of ventriloquism—a skill that, it should be known, a scientific debunker also once invoked to explain away Edison's phonograph.

It is said that a beloved American ventriloquist, Edgar Bergen, related to his puppet character, Charley Macarthy, as though the little guy was a real person. The ventriloquist once remarked, in apparent sincerity, that the puppet was one of the wisest people he knew. By this we can assume he meant that he knew very well that he was creating the voice of his puppet character, but that he was aware of something larger than him supplying the words that this character would say.

This phenomenon bears a prima facie resemblance to channeling, which has, in its various forms, long been the rage among us aficionados of the paranormal.

Reflections on the Mirror

Mirrors are another important interface between the entertainment world and the world of the paranormal. Long before stage illusionists amused the public with them, mirrors were regarded as objects of supernatural significance. That ancient idea stemmed from the Mirror Vision Complex, a normal psychological condition consisting of a constellation of highly curious phenomena of consciousness that are associated with reflections.

Many people are susceptible to extraordinary visionary experiences when gazing into the clear optical depths of a mirror. These visions are unlike ordinary reflections, though the medium that creates the reflection may be the same, and they seem to have a life of their own. Typically, a gazer first sees clouds, mists, fog, or smoke, and immediately thereafter the visions themselves commence. Mirror visions are eidetic; that is, they appear to the observer as though they were located in external space, within the observer's visual field, but originating deep within the mirror itself.

Mirror visions usually are iridescently colored and fully three-dimensional. They move in a natural way, like characters or events seen in a movie. The content of the visions falls into several categories:

1. People whom the gazer knows and others whom the gazer does not recognize

2. Panoramic scenes of preternatural beauty, such as lakes, forests, and mountain ranges

3. Minidramas involving several people within a unified setting engaged in some activity

4. Forgotten or dimly remembered incidents of the gazer's early life, vividly resurrected

The apparent size of the visionary figures is in keeping with the size of the mirror, minute images being seen in small mirrors, large images in large ones. The visions do not always confine themselves to the mirror, however; sometimes they appear to merge into the surrounding environment. The gazer may also experience a sensation of going through the mirror into an alternate, three-dimensional, visionary world.

Mirror visions may surprise the observer by appearing spontaneously, or a gazer may precipitate them by peering into a mirror in the expectation or hope of seeing them. In either case, there is a sense that the visions appear and play themselves out independently of the gazer's conscious will.

People who take up mirror gazing as a continuing spiritual practice (or for creative inspiration, as some artists and writers do) may experience further developments of the Mirror Vision Complex.

The mirror has been a natural symbol of the self since antiquity, and the use of the word *reflection* to describe both an outward optical effect and an inward process of self-discovery embodies this same metaphor. Perhaps that is why it often seems to people who devote themselves to mirror gazing that the circumstances under which they acquire their mirrors are of supernatural significance; these gazers relate tales of finding their treasured mirrors through the agency of coincidences so unlikely as to seem themselves paranormally preordained.

In ancient and medieval times, it was generally believed that an indwelling spirit produced the visions seen in a mirror. Firsthand accounts by today's seasoned mirror gazers suggest that this old belief derived from an actual phenomenon of consciousness. A veteran gazer may report that the same spiritual being repeatedly appears in the mirror on many separate occasions. The mirror entity acts as a moderator, directing the rest of the visionary show that the gazer sees.

Mirror visions can be seen in other types of speculums, too. Other reflective or transparent surfaces, objects, or substances serve just as well. Gazers have used quartz crystals, bowls, or other vessels filled with ink or oil, and the still, clear waters of ponds or lakes.

However odd the Mirror Vision Complex may seem upon first hearing about it, it is a perfectly normal psychological faculty, and it is widely distributed in the general population. Each component element of the Mirror Vision Complex shows up, too, in an abundance of myths and legends, fairy tales and folklore, from diverse cultures all over the world.

Snow White's evil stepmother peers into her "mirror, mirror on the wall" to find out who is fairest of all. Aladdin and his mother are surprised to see a wishing-genie pop out of the reflective surface of a brass lamp she has just polished. There are hundreds of other traditional tales with similar mirror visionary themes. Obviously, the Mirror Vision Complex has a great deal of potential as pure entertainment.

Just as clearly, mirror visions are behind numerous familiar phenomena that are conceptualized as paranormal. The best-known of these is called "scrying," which is divination by the interpretation of mirror visions. In antiquity, the rulers of far-flung empires employed court diviners, who used magic mirrors to view what was happening in distant corners of their realms. Apache medicine men "scryed" in quartz crystals, Cherokees in clear lakes, and Aztecs in mirrors of polished obsidian.

Genesis says that Joseph had a "silver cup, in which he divineth," a practice that is still current in the Middle East. Polished silver cups or bowls are filled with olive oil for the purpose. Ezekiel saw his prophetic visions in the waters of the River Chebar. The chief prophet of Tibet peered into a metal mirror, and cabinet ministers took his visions into account in determining state policy.

In medieval Europe, the seers, or *specularii*, traveled from town to town telling fortunes and helping to locate lost objects by gazing into mirrors.

And as recently as a century ago, scientists who were trying to formulate canons for systematically investigating apparitions of the deceased compiled compendia of accounts by supposedly articulate and reliable witnesses. In a significant proportion of the cases, the respondents first saw the apparitions in mirrors or other reflective or transparent objects or surfaces.

In my own work (which seems like it was in the nineteenth century, but has really been in the past twenty years), I have interviewed about two dozen people who saw spontaneous mirror visions of departed relatives or friends.

If we let the little children lead us, we will come full circle back to the theme of play and the paranormal. There is a childhood parlor game of altered consciousness in which, after performing varying rituals, kids gaze into a mirror to see a ghost. So, the little ones sense that it is possible to "call spirits from the vasty deep."

Mirrors are, of course, a standard prop in stage magic. They are also an essential component of popular toys, including kaleidoscopes. People like to laugh at their own too-fat or too-thin images in distorting mirrors at carnivals or boardwalks. And mirror mazes are old standbys at amusement parks and in funhouses.

The reputation of mirror visions has suffered greatly from their popular association with fortune telling. Convention openly countenances derisive laughter at divination by crystal gazing. The gypsy woman peering into her crystal ball is a customary target of magazine cartoon caricature.

From the Sublime to the Ridiculous

Sometimes, after all, the paranormal is just funny, as the wacky saga of the piss prophets reveals.

The practitioners of that antique health profession diagnosed human disease and prognosticated as to its outcome by interpreting the visions they saw when they gazed into glass flasks of their patients' urine. They enjoyed enormous respect in Europe from early in the fourteenth century until several hundred years later. At the height of their popularity, they employed helpers known as piss messengers, who fetched urine from the homes of the bedridden and delivered it to the prophet for his inspection and pronouncement.

For a time during the medieval period, the piss prophet's glass flask was the recognized emblem of the medical profession. It was always pictured as either half empty or half full, depending on which way you looked at it. Carried in its protective wicker basket, it was worn as the outwardly visible badge of the medical doctor.

Piss prophets were always at war with debunkers who tried to trick the practitioners by substituting animal urine for human. In the late eighteenth century, the last fashionable uroscopist in England was laughed out of practice. He had pronounced that a young man had venereal disease on the basis of a flask of cow's urine submitted to him by hoaxers.

Wishing wells, now a pop icon of superstition, were once a popular paranormal institution derived from mirror gazing practices. People thought that a spirit inhabited a wishing well, and, originally, petitioners visualized the spirit in the waters below. Wishers tossed coins in to bribe the well genie.

Still Another Connection between the Paranormal and Entertainment: The Mysterious Maze

Printed maze puzzles are a universally recognized type of plaything for children and for adults alike. They are published by the hundreds every year. In the 1990s a big craze developed for walking through enormous wall mazes that took about ninety minutes to negotiate.

Mazes and labyrinths were big draws in antiquity, too. The vast labyrinth in Egypt was the prototype of four such structures in the ancient world. Herodotus reported that the Egyptian labyrinth was near the place called the City of Crocodiles. I have seen this building, and it is beyond my power to describe; it must have cost more in labour and money than all the walls and public works of the Greeks put together. . . . The pyramids, too, are astonishing structures, each one of them equal to many of the most ambitious works of Greece; but the labyrinth surpasses them. It has twelve covered courts—six in a row facing north, six south—the gates of the one range exactly fronting the gates of the other, with a continuous wall round the outside of the whole. Inside, the building is of two storeys and contains three thousand rooms, of which half are underground, and the other half directly above them. I was taken through the rooms in the upper storey only, and it is hard to believe that they are the work of men; the baffling and intricate passages from room to room and from court to court were an endless wonder to me, as we passed from a courtyard into rooms, from rooms into galleries, from galleries into more rooms, and thence into yet more courtyards. The roof of every chamber, courtyard, and gallery is, like the walls, of stone. The walls are covered with carved figures, and each court is exquisitely built of white marble and surrounded by a colonnade. Near the corner where the labyrinth ends there is a pyramid, two hundred and forty feet in height, with great carved figures of animals on it.

The labyrinth's designers honeycombed it with optical illusions. At every turn, doors in the walls deceptively suggested the way ahead, only to shepherd the treaders right back over their own tracks. The building was engineered acoustically so that every time the outer doors were opened a terrifying sound like thunder rumbled within. Once led inside, no stranger could find the way out without a guide.

No one knows why the ancient labyrinths were built, but they became major tourist attractions. It is clear that mazes and labyrinths have long been linked with the supernatural in mythology and in rituals recorded by ethnographers. In some myths, fearsome preternatural monsters inhabited labyrinths. The Greeks said that the Minotaur—half man, half bull—lived in the Cretan labyrinth. He murdered scores of young Athenians, who were imprisoned in the labyrinth as sacrificial victims. Theseus managed to kill the Minotaur and then to find his way out again, guided by the ball of thread he had unraveled behind him on his way in.

The belief that mazes and labyrinths have magical or paranormal properties has persisted from primordial times to the present. Norse fishermen built stone labyrinths along the shores of the Baltic Sea. They raced through the structures before setting out on fishing trips in the belief that any evil spirits that were trying to follow them would be trapped in the labyrinths' complicated turns. The fishermen walked through the labyrinths in procession in order paranormally to guarantee good sailing weather or a bountiful catch.

Wandering through a maze of blind alleys, branch points, crisscrosses, dead ends, and ambages can bend a treader's mind. Wall mazes lack symmetry and pattern and are high enough to prevent the treader from seeing where he is. Such classic maze characteristics can add up to a severe case of befuddlement, disorientation, and fear of entrapment, all pretty amazing feelings.

Lots of fans of paranormal mystery still feel that there is something distinctly otherworldly about wandering around in mazes. *Maze* and *labyrinth* actually mean the same thing, but a few enthusiasts distinguish the two by using *labyrinth* to refer only to the familiar coiled, unicursal maze. Often, that kind of labyrinth is built with low walls that do not constrict the vision as wall mazes do. People who try both kinds say that the two provide treaders with two different kinds of experiences. Those who walk through the gradually spiraling, coiled, unicursal labyrinths tend to say that the experience "centers" them, and among us contemporary devotees of the paranormal, that is a very fashionable kind of thing to say.

Children and the Paranormal:
Toys and Games, or Tools and Rituals?

Various kinds of toys have been used to create paranormal effects. Nowadays, almost every child has played with a bull roarer; ancient shamans zoomed themselves into altered states of consciousness with the awesome sound produced by these devices, and their use was surrounded with ritual. The aboriginal shamans of Australia used bull roarers to ascend into the spirit world, with the entire arrangement—medicine man plus whirling implement—making up a sort of astral helicopter. So, as Lang asks: "Was the thing originally a toy, and is its religious and mystical nature later; or was it originally one of the properties of the priest, or medicine-man, which in [contemporary Western society] has dwindled to a plaything?"

Today, children delight in wearing masks on Halloween and to costume parties; in earlier times, masks were worn ceremonially in connection with otherworld journeys and other shamanic adventures. Like shamans, little tots shake rattles and pound on drums.

And just what is the status of kids' imaginary playmates? Do the unseen companions of the very young partake more of fun or of the phenomenal, of amusement or of apparition, of jubilation or of juju?

Little ones don't have to be taught to twirl themselves around and around into strange states of dizzy exaltation. They learn to do it by themselves, early in their lives. But it's not just kids who learn to love ecstatic spinning. In the twelfth century, the mystical poet Rumi turned child's play into a revolution in paranormal consciousness when he founded the first circle of Sufi Whirling Dervishes. The Persian word *darwish* meant "seeking doors," so the Whirling Dervishes rotated in order to enter other realms. Photographs plainly reveal that the whirlers pirouette themselves into ecstatic states of consciousness.

When, as is necessary for the purpose of systematic inquiry, the subject matter of the paranormal is subdivided into its various parts, constituents, or elements, a few of the sub-components that turn up can plausibly be categorized as hobbies. The perdurable avocation of the Nostradamians, for example, has much in common with the popular hobby of working word puzzles such as acrostics and crossword puzzles.

The Nostradamus Nostrum

It has become a nostrum among the *cognicenti paranormalae* that Nostradamus was a man of great wisdom and insight, and a seer of the first rank. Indeed, the word *nostrum* itself provides ample evidence of this individual's impact on our culture. Nostradamus (1503–1566) took an interest in entertaining, at least in one sense, because his first published work was a collection of recipes for tasty dishes and facial makeup compounds—a cookbook, in fact, although surprisingly it contained no directions for baking fortune cookies. Even during his lifetime, he was widely hailed as a prophet, and the legend persists that he was a visionary who peered into the future by means of catoptromancy (divination by mirror gazing). That tradition rests on very slim evidence, however.

Whatever means Nostradamus might have used to induce his visions, if indeed he had visions, what we are left with as his prophetic work is a collection of verses that are in no way obviously connected with mirror visions. In the long term, it has been through these quatrains that he has acquired his reputation for prodigious feats of precognition. From our earliest years, we are taught diligently to seek the meaning in verse, so many a reader is already on the seer's side, ever on the alert to interpret the words in accordance with the abiding convention that they allude to important world events that Nostradamus foresaw. However, the verses whip up such a fine, fuzzy fog of ambiguity that they are capable of interpretation and reinterpretation without limit. The words trip deftly along the shifting edges of meaningfulness, tantalizing because their meaning seems forever to lie just beyond the reach of comprehension. What Nostradamus left behind—a fermat's last theorem of futurity—is really a pastime, a continuing legacy of admirers indulging themselves in a hobby, reading and rereading the fabled lines as if in search of the one, true solution to an enduring puzzle.

Closing the Case: Play and the Paranormal

Viewed panoramically, all the foregoing paranormal "funomena" are evidence that there is an intrinsic affiliation between the paranormal and entertainment, or recreational activity. So, a proper, serious, meticulous paranormalist would begin by recognizing in the social and cultural phenomenon that is the paranormal a major form of popular entertainment and amusement, a divertissement of great antiquity, and of sublime historical and psychological significance.

Those who believe in the paranormal should not be put off by this idea, but turned on! For this understanding of our collective human back story can be the basis of an alternate take on the subject, an avowedly playful paranormalist view, to be sure, but a view which could very well open new windows on the paranormal, and lead us to new understandings of it.

It is my proposition that the reason we do not more fully understand the paranormal is that we have been approaching it, looking at it, and talking about it in the same way for hundreds of years. It is time for a new approach.

To be taken seriously, however, playful paranormalists must get their act together by refusing to take any of the old standby positions that proponents of the three off-the-shelf theories have always taken. Then the serious, scholarly, playful paranormalists can get their own show on the road by presenting a documentary of how and why those three well-known companies of performers—the three categories of people who have been the only ones allowed to discuss the paranormal under the old ground rules—stage the continuing show that comprises their familiar tripolar controversy about this subject.

In other words, if we are willing to take the subject not quite so seriously (perhaps by noticing that the subject itself has been well grounded in play and entertainment), we just might be able to expand what has heretofore been exclusively a three-part trialogue on this subject. We may even break up the logjam that has characterized it.

3

BREAKING UP THE LOGJAM: UNRIDDLING THE CONTROVERSY ABOUT THE PARANORMAL

Most people are satisfied that they know how to reason about the paranormal. That is to say, they are complacent about the standard operating procedure for disputing such phenomena that have been handed down from antiquity. People usually accept that the battle lines are to be drawn between the yea-sayers and the naysayers, between those who believe and those who are skeptical. They are aware that it is customary to enter the controversy by taking up a side—the affirmative or the negative. This is the unwritten law of argumentation about the paranormal by which the people keep even the "experts" on the subject in awe.

Almost everyone concerned is well pleased with the prescriptive framework of controversy, or at least they silently acquiesce in it. They assume that the traditional game plan is commensurate with the task of establishing the truth about the paranormal. After all, it has been broken in by more than twenty centuries of scholars, pro and con; interested laypersons accede to it, too. It keeps on running by force of habit, and each generation of devotees of the subject inculcates it in the next.

As a playful paranormalist, I am now making it known that I reject that entire master plan of disputation. The old system of guidelines for disceptation is petrified; it is inapt and inept. It is sustained only by the antiquity of its errors. The whole system is a ponderous, reactionary bureaucracy that effectively stonewalls progress in the understanding of one of the most fascinating dimensions of human consciousness.

It is time to break up the logjam. Again, I submit that this is going to require a new, playful attitude about that which itself is so deeply rooted in play and entertainment. It is time for a little "playful paranormalism."

Now I want you to know that this is not a middle-of-the-road, wishy-washy position! I am not going to straddle any fences. Playful paranormalist shouldn't be misunderstood to be waffling, agnostic compromisers. I am not setting out playful paranormalism as a way of bringing all those mismatched brawlers together under the same umbrella.

Playful paranormalism is no middling, fourth-rate attempt at pleasing everyone. I wouldn't endeavor to transform the old triangular controversy into a new, exclusive quaternity, either. No, a playful paranormalist should be above all that, and I espouse a far more radical point of view.

Playful paranormalists are of the opinion that the only viable option available to scholars who want to make headway in the study of paranormal phenomena, and break up the logjam around it, is backing away from that entire, rickety old edifice of argumentation, identifying its critical weak points, and then blowing the whole thing apart.

This will be a lengthy undertaking. It should probably only be undertaken by "serious students" of the "playful."

Opening the New Dialogue: A Playful Look at the Serious

I will begin it by focusing on three equally irrational creeds, which I categorized earlier—that of the parapsychologist, the skeptic, and the fundamentalist—in a way that shows that each can plausibly be accounted for under the playful paranormalist's basic argument that there is an equation of the paranormal with entertainment.

Most logomachy about the paranormal is carried on by the above three distinct kinds of thick-witted triflers. These triflers indulge themselves in three correspondingly distinct ways of convincing themselves that they are in possession of the truth about the paranormal, or that they know the correct way of getting at the truth.

Category 1: Parapsychologists

Especially insofar as it is favorably disposed to the notion of a life after death, parapsychology (category 1) can be construed as a form of comedy, in that it attempts to assure, or to reassure, us that life has a happy ending. Furthermore, since tragedy is contrasted with comedy in that tragedy ends in death, parapsychology represents a high order of the comic spirit by seeking to establish that even death, the culmination of tragedy, has a happy outcome.

Category 2: Skeptics

The skeptics (category 2) dismiss the claim of parapsychology to be a science; and playful paranormalism is similarly dubious that science as we know it could prove life after death, precognition, and so on. To a playful paranormalist, it seems a peculiar notion that there would be a science of which the chief activity and goal is to prove the existence of the very phenomena with which it purports to deal. The skeptics have failed to realize the full significance of this, for they cast themselves in the role of the scientific rivals of the parapsychologists. But these debunkers actually play a different role in the dynamics of the controversy about the paranormal. If parapsychology is a form of comedy, then a skeptical debunker of the paranormal is more like a heckler at the performance of a comedian, a person who spoils the fun.

Playful paranormalists respectfully acknowledge the role that members of the Committee for the Scientific Investigation of Claims of the Paranormal play in keeping the discussion honest, but we cannot pass lightly over the fact that, while their formal name mentions science and inquiry, members are in the habit of referring to themselves by the acronym CSICOPs (Get it?), a nickname that betrays a sinister, authoritarian design. They aspire to be the reality police, vested with the power of ruling on the ontological status of other people's experiences.

Consequently, their interpersonal style leaves a lot to be desired. What impresses me, upon reading their literature and from appearing with them on television programs, is that, like their counterparts in the audiences of nightclub comedians, what skeptical hecklers crave is more attention for themselves. They do a great deal of complaining, whining, and sighing about how little press coverage or talk show time they get compared to what they believe they deserve. That's why playful paranormalists refer to CSICOPs as the "sigh cops."

And what happens if a sigh cop catches you? Is there an entire sigh justice system? Are there sigh judges and sigh juries, too, or do the sigh cops bring you to trial and sentence you themselves? And how do sigh cops reconcile science with the image of their being empowered to round up offenders?

The self-proclaimed skeptics are not skeptical enough. If they were, they would pursue their inquiries further, into the deeper, underlying problems of philosophy. The questions of the paranormal (that is, whether ESP, foreknowledge, or an after-death world exist) are only fuzzily stated, awkward misformulations of issues that have kept philosophers busy for twenty centuries. There can be no solution of the supposed problem of whether there is a life after death outside of a solution of the larger philosophical dilemma known as the mind-body problem. Alleged issues of the existence of telepathy and precognition beg more subtle, more complex questions of epistemology (the theory of knowledge).

The truth is, the sigh cops are not skeptics at all. They are ideologues who think they have the answers. The ideology they swear by is known as *scientism,* the belief that the methods and assumptions of the natural sciences are the only ones appropriate for the pursuit of knowledge. *Scientism* is a value judgment that other disciplines—philosophy, the humanities, and the social sciences—are worthwhile only insofar as they conform their techniques of investigation to those of the physical and biological sciences.

It is a misnomer for the skeptics to refer to themselves as the Committee for the *Scientific* Investigation of Claims of the Paranormal. *Scientistic* is the word they are looking for.

The sigh cops have a vested interest in keeping the discussion of the paranormal on a superficial level. Playful paranormalism is by far a more skeptical position about the paranormal than sigh copism is.

The sigh cops present themselves as undertaking a scientific enterprise, but they are really conducting a social crusade. Ultimately, what the skeptics fear (and this by their own admission) is that if people in modern society are allowed to take the paranormal seriously, then they will quickly revert to witchcraft trials and burnings. If this is so, then it is paradoxical that "sigh cops" exhaust so much of their ammunition in battles with the parapsychologists. The funda-Christians seem the more likely suspects in that sort of crime.

Category 3: Fundamentalists

What has been uncovered goes a long way toward enabling us to understand why fundamentalists (category 3) so abhor the paranormal; things that smack of fun are not their forte. This is the same group, remember, that throughout American history has agitated in favor of banning many other popular forms of entertainment: dancing, jazz, movies that are too sexy, movies on Sunday, movies anytime, and rock 'n' roll music.

Fundamentalists of whatever stripe, whether they refer to themselves as Christians or Jews, Muslims or Marxists, are at bottom the same (get it?).

(Listen, it is important for you to get the humor here if you are to be a card-carrying playful paranormalist).

Dour and humorless, fundamentalists are preoccupied with ideology. Since universal ideological conformity is likely to remain forever impossible, however, fundamentalism by its nature requires an enemy, an out-group to contrast with the in-group. The ideology must provide an undesirable fate for those who do not conform; they must burn in hell, or end up in the dust bin of history!

Some Christian fundamentalists don't like to be referred to as fundamentalists, so they hide out under an alias of their own choosing, ducking for cover under some other qualifying term. The word *fundamentalist* makes them uneasy, because it calls attention to how closely their impudent, judgmental personalities resemble those of the advocates of other mean-minded persuasions. Simplistic bigots of every sect have to make a special exception for themselves. How else would they be able to rationalize their hate-mongering against freethinkers, nonbelievers, homosexuals, political or social liberals, heretics, people who are interested in the paranormal, Mormons, or any other groups of human beings they target?

The key to understanding funda-Christians, their predilection for matters of ideology, their stern aversion to levity, and their preoccupation with the demonic, is in identifying their underlying psychological style—the mind-set of obsession.

The features the funda-Christians attribute to demons coincide with the concerns of those afflicted by obsessions. Demons are said to attempt to deceive their victims, perhaps by appearing in disguise; intrusive, persistent doubt is a hallmark of the obsessional frame of mind. Demons are characterized as foul, filthy, and dirty, and they are associated with disgusting smells; cleanliness and purity are well-known preoccupations of obsessives. Belief in demons has a built-in action component, in that demons are to be avoided, exorcised, or warded off, usually by rituals; obsessions tend to be acted out in the form of compulsions, rituals performed with the intent of avoiding, cleaning, or warding off.

Obsessional tendencies have been related to anal fixation. If you've watched their antics on television, can you deny that funda-Christians appear to be straining at stool as they pray? Their heads down, eyes squeezed tightly shut, their faces screw up with intensity as they stammer, " . . . JAY-us . . . uhn . . . uhn . . . JAY-zus . . . uhn . . . uhn."

The lifestyle preferred by obsessive-compulsives is one of dreary sameness. A content analysis of evening television commercials reveals how partial they are to regularity. Innovation is the bane of the fundamentalists' existence, because it presents continual challenges to ideology. That is why they attribute so many novel ideas or contrivances to the devil.

Funda-Christians who map the paranormal dimensions of consciousness are like the medieval cartographers who drew to the limits of their knowledge, and beyond that added the legend: "Here be dragons." Even the dinner fork was derided as Satanic when it was invented, and priestly know-it-alls told Galileo that he was being deceived by demonic visions when he first viewed distant planets through his telescope. So, for a playful paranormalist, it is a positive development to hear humorless old you-know-who's griping that something we are prying into is of the devil, for that is a sure clue there may be something fun and interesting in it.

Listening casually to the oraculations of funda-Christians, one could easily be taken in by the illusion that they are exact in their manner of thinking and speaking. Exactly what God is to be believed to have meant by exactly which word or verse in that exact translation of the Bible is to be believed exactly as each speaking believer believes God meant every last one of us to believe it. Listening more attentively, though, the exactitude of funda-Christian thought and speech, it turns out, is not a matter of its being exact, but, rather, a matter of its being exacting. And an exacting manner of speaking and thinking is exactly what one expects boorishly obsessional folks would have.

Obsessional people focus on abstractions as a way of isolating themselves from feelings and emotions. This explains why ideology is the centerpiece of religion for funda-Christians. It explains, too, their dour humorlessness and the attitude that, historically, they have taken to entertainment. It is well known that obsessive-compulsives are relatively immune to mirth. If they hear an amusing story or joke, they often misinterpret it as a serious remark and take issue with its literal meaning. What passes for humor among such persons often takes the form of biting, hostile wit, or tight-lipped sarcasm. Since hearty laughter implies surrender of control, it is especially threatening for fundamentalist types, since they defend themselves with their rigidity.

This enables us precisely to identify those who, while praising themselves as Christians, actually are only menacing other people with threats of devils. Since demonology is defined as belief in demons, funda-Christians are, more specifically, demonologists. And the major trouble with demonologists has always been that they become so good at spotting demons and get so good at seeing the demons running around in other people's lives and at positively identifying other people's demons in the line-up, that the demonologists don't do much delving into their own demons. And that is why fundamentalists' private demons so regularly unleash themselves and run rampant over other folks' rights.

This analysis convincingly and authentically pegs the three official theories, characterizing the parts they play in the standard controversy by placing each set of ideas within a framework of the concepts of humor and entertainment. This powerfully reinforces the barrage of specific examples that already has linked the paranormal with the performing arts. However, there is a still more direct way to reveal that the element of fun is at the heart of the paranormal. All we have to do is listen to the way people talk about it.

4

MIRACLES, MEANINGS, AND MERRIMENT

This chapter has to do with words. Specifically, the words that we use today to discuss the paranormal.

What I am suggesting throughout this whole book is that, if we are to discover any real truths about the paranormal, about near-death experiences, and about life after death, we will only do so if we stop taking everything *so seriously*. By that I mean, we must stop taking everything we think we know about these subjects *so literally*. Because—whether trying to learn more about the paranormal; trying to learn more about God and religion (Be careful! these might be one and the same thing!); trying to learn more about politics, or economics, or human sexuality; or trying to learn more about *anything*—taking things *literally* is precisely what has impeded that learning.

Neale Donald Walsch says he was told in his *Conversations with God* that "words are the least reliable form of communication." Now if we are stuck on trying to decide whether it is *literally* true that Walsch talked to God, we will miss completely the meaning of what was said. This is a prime example of how insisting on literal meaning—that is, taking things so seriously that we make no room whatsoever for discovery, but insist that the Truth, the Whole Truth, and Nothing But the Truth must be, and is, contained in the words themselves, as literally understood—obscures meaning altogether.

The playful paranormalist is inclined to look past the question of whether an actual communication with Deity took place (a question that can never be resolved in any event), and to look instead at whether there is anything of wisdom and value in the communication that was received. The playful paranormalist is willing to "play with the idea" that Walsch *might* have talked with God, and then ask: If he did, would it not be interesting to see what God had to say?

I am suggesting here, therefore, that there be established a whole new category of "discussers" on topics paranormal. Henceforth on talk shows, in books and published articles, and around coffee tables all over America and around the world, we need not be limited to (1) the parapsychologists, (2) the professional skeptics, or (3) the fundamentalists. Now we can add to the table (4) the playful paranormalists.

We've got to broaden the discussion precisely because the discussion so far has gotten us nowhere. We have reached a stalemate. We've created that logjam. And playing with ideas, rather than taking them so seriously that we insist on considering what we hear to be literally true, is the only approach that will end the cat's game.

The reason I am devoting a whole chapter to words and how we use them is to demonstrate why we've got to stop using them as our only tool of discovery about the paranormal, and begin using ideas as well. I am going to demonstrate that the words-alone approach to understanding the paranormal (or *anything)* can lead us to only conclude that the paranormal is, quite literally, nonsense. After I have demonstrated this, playful paranormalism will have thoroughly justified itself as a novel, systematic approach to exploring these topics, in which all of us have such a great interest.

All of that having been said, you might still ask, why this particular left turn in the book? Is this look at words and how we use them to discuss "the paranormal" really important? Yes. Aren't we talking about mere semantics here? No.

Words, gathered together as firsthand accounts of other-worldly experiences, or published as reports of seemingly supernatural occurrences, have heretofore made up the major part of what students and investigators of the paranormal go on as they strive to unravel its mysteries. This sharply contrasts with the situation that prevails in many a more respectable discipline—chemistry or biology or geography or whatever. In those disciplines, one uses direct observation of physical phenomena, and the ideas to which such observations lead us. With the paranormal, observational additional data are rarely available. So words form the chief information resource, and thus, how we say things, what languaging we use, becomes an all-important matter.

For example, is there a difference in nuance between the words *paranormal, superstition,* and *occult*? You bet your life there is. Do those differences color the way the topic is discussed? Of course they do. The words we use set the tone of the dialogue. They establish the parameters. That is the very point I am making.

Words being a key to what we presently think we know about the paranormal, all of us astute experts on the subject must pay close attention to words and their meanings, and we must begin by surveying the present basic vocabulary of the paranormal.

Beginning at the Beginning

The first of the mysteries of the paranormal is the meaning of the word *paranormal. Meaning* itself being a word with no one meaning, and theories about how words have their meanings being numerous and contending, it will be helpful to pin down the meaning of *paranormal* not just in one, but in several, related meanings of *meaning*.

(Already you can see that only a playful paranormalist would even be willing to undertake such an exercise. One has to be playful about this. Insistent literalists lose patience too quickly. So, let us playful paranormalists proceed.)

The best dictionaries succeed only in making a frail and tenuous kind of sense of the word, the most that lexicographers are able to do in the way of getting down to a precise meaning amidst a welter of verbiage. It is said that *paranormal* designates powers or phenomena that operate outside what are said to be the known laws of nature or "normal objective investigation." But since there is no clear sense in which powers or phenomena can be said to be spatially outside the laws of nature or spatially outside a particular method of investigation, it is not a literal sense but, rather a figurative sense, of "outside" that is put forward here. Surely it is highly suspicious that a spatial metaphor would play so crucial a role in the definition.

Other dictionary makers approach the problem differently, specifying that the word *paranormal* pertains to purported "events or perceptions that are without scientific explanation." The word *without* is also, in part, a spatial metaphor, but here at least the definition can be recast as "events or perceptions for which there is no scientific explanation," a phrase that is clear enough, but seems to say more about what the paranormal is not than about what it is. Furthermore, there are plenty of scientifically unexplained events or perceptions that no one would count as paranormal.

The problem is not just that there is a figure of speech at the core of the definition of *paranormal,* but that the figure of speech is one for which no clear literal equivalent can be specified. This leads the insistent literalist straight into confusion. For when the definer is pressed to substitute a clear literal meaning for that figure of speech, he or she invariably resorts to specifying only what the paranormal is *not!* And specifying what something is *not* is failing to define it at all.

Thus, to this point (and this is precisely what has created the logjam), definitions of *paranormal* have oscillated between obscurely *figurative* language and uninformative *negative* language. That oscillation has produced *literal* nonsense. That is, something that makes no sense, literally, at all.

Now if we conclude that a thing makes no sense, how in the world can we sensibly discuss it? The answer is, of course, that we cannot—which is exactly why the discussion has reached a stalemate.

A Solution to This Dilemma

There is a way out of this vicious cycle, however. One dictionary attempts to plug the gaping holes in its definition of *paranormal* by offering a synonym—*supernatural.* By looking up *supernatural* and then looking up any synonyms in terms of which it is defined, it is possible to follow a trail of synonyms and near-synonyms, until at last the net begins to close back on itself as the words begin to repeat themselves.

Proceeding in this way, a whole family of related expressions eventually can be identified, and this family of words and meanings turns out to be something really workable for the purposes of a playful paranormalist.

Here is a partial list, but a representative one: paranormal, supernatural, preternatural, extramundane, otherworldly, ethereal, unseen, strange, spooky, weird, eerie, hyperphysical, bizarre, wacky, goofy, mumbo jumbo, incredible, unbelievable, extraordinary, miracles, wonders, anomalies, marvels, ghostly, spectral, hocus-pocus, unearthly, metaphysical, occult, uncanny, abnormal, parapsychology, parascience, superstition, unknown.

This thicket of terminology can be reduced to several discernible categories of expressions.

There are words that designate or describe something by setting it apart from what is known (occult, uncanny, strange, unknown) or from what is known by some particular way or method of knowing (unseen, paranormal, parapsychology, parascience).

There are terms that designate or describe something by setting it apart from some other norm or standard than knowledge. That other norm or standard may be nature (supernatural, preternatural, miracles), or the substantial or material (ghostly, spooky, spectral, ethereal), or law (anomalies), or the ordinary (extraordinary), or the normal (abnormal, paranormal), or what can be believed (incredible, unbelievable), or what should be believed (superstition), or what is local (strange), or even the entire world (extramundane, otherworldly, unearthly).

There are expressions that characterize this unknown, or otherwise set-apart, something in terms of an effect it has on consciousness. This effect may be one of exciting wonder (marvels, wonders, strange), or of being disturbingly odd (eerie, weird, bizarre, uncanny), or of inducing fear (spooky, superstition).

There are some terms that also often are used to impute mental disorder (bizarre, abnormal, weird), often expressed as the humorously deviant (wacky, goofy).

And there are expressions that make fun of this unknown, or otherwise set-apart, something as positively nonsensical (hocus-pocus, mumbo jumbo).

It is not necessary that any two of the terms that make up this cluster of words and meanings be strictly synonymous. Rather, their differences in meaning may be every bit as interesting and important as their similarities in meaning. All eerie or bizarre things are strange, for example, but not all strange things are eerie or bizarre. Nor can every one of the words be counted on to have the same degree or kind of bearing on the paranormal in each and every context of its usage. And, who knows, that consideration could someday conceivably make a practical difference in some specific context or other. A weird or bizarre person asking for help might well be packed off to a mental hospital, for example, while an eerie person in need of assistance would perhaps be more likely to be directed to a parapsychologist's office.

What is more, a number of the words fit into more than one of the categories (paranormal, strange, spooky, uncanny, superstition). These interconnections have the effect of interweaving all the words and their meanings into a lush, linguistic tapestry of intense, emotional dynamism.

Does Any of This Really Matter?

As playful paranormalists, we are having a bit of fun looking lightheartedly at this problem of words—we are exploring ideas playfully—but, as I have said before, there is a problem here, make no mistake about that. Because this fabric of interdefined words and meanings is so strongly charged emotionally, it has become highly politicized.

Each of the three off-the-shelf ways of construing the paranormal (categories 1, 2 and 3, as discussed above) nurses its own grievances, and each harbors its own aspirations. The members of each category have become insistent literalists, and it is in keeping with their own specific gripes and yearnings that each picks and chooses its own favorite word from all those that are available. Having chosen a word, they then take it literally. They may even trump up new words with stipulated meanings that are congruent with their own sentiments and preoccupations.

It is in this way that our three original groups have managed to continue the discussion without continuing the exploration. That is, they have managed to keep a conversation going without letting it get anywhere. Let's look at how these insistent literalists have done this.

How Category 1 Languages the Paranormal

Paranormal itself is that kind of innovative coinage, a contrivance typical of the parapsychological mind-set. Parapsychologists (category 1) incessantly grumble about the unfair treatment they feel they receive from the scientific community. They wish to be recognized as scientists and to be accorded the respect that scientists enjoy.

The word *paranormal* was duly concocted to cater to those hankerings by narrowing down the meanings present in an entire plexus of terminology to those that have specifically to do with knowledge and that have even more specifically to do with the kind of knowledge that is the province of science.

All the unserious or otherwise bothersome connotations that might embarrass serious scientists or other weighty scholars were discarded from the richer body of meanings. The framers of *paranormal* edited out all the humorous nuances and put a halt to all of the teasing. They excised the unsettling effects on consciousness and also the inspiring and elevating ones. This parapsychologists' neoparanormal was not going to put up with anymore of its own nonsense, and it neglected to mention the madness that runs in its family.

This bid to seize academic respectability by linguistic fiat presupposed that the only way to bring the study of the paranormal into the mainstream would be to make it a branch of science. But how could it be determined, prior to a full and impartial hearing, that creditable university paranormalists would belong more properly in the science building than across the campus with historians, philosophers, psychologists, or specialists in literary or religious studies, or even in the drama department?

Learned professionals from many august disciplines would have solid grounds for objecting to the framers' presumption that science is the "normal" way of knowing. It could be argued with equal plausibility that science is a decidedly non-normal way of knowing.

Why, then, was the word "normal" introduced as a stand-in for "scientific knowledge" in the first place? Whether they were fully aware of it or not, those who originally stipulated the meaning of *paranormal* had to refrain from referring straightforwardly to scientific knowledge. By getting too close to the desired meaning, they would have negated it.

This can be made painfully obvious by substituting a term that unambiguously designates scientific knowledge as *normal* in *paranormal,* as did the inventors of the word parascience. This ill-fated expression was meant to mean "the scientific knowledge of that which lies beyond scientific knowledge"—an overt self-contradiction!

Another grave non sequitur is concealed in the thought that legitimizing the subject for serious scientific or scholarly consideration requires doing away with the light side of the paranormal. In part, this is a play on the notion of seriousness: humor is not serious; hence, humor is not a topic fit for serious scientific or scholarly concern.

When it is clearly formulated thus, the argument is transparently fallacious. In its insidiously unstated form, though, it has served as a powerful deterrent to the systematic investigation of mirth. I believe that it has also retarded the systematic investigation of the paranormal.

And all the parapsychologists' verbal finagling came to naught anyway! As it leaked out of the technical jargon of serious parapsychologists into popular usage, the word *paranormal* gathered back to itself all those obnoxious sideshow meanings that the founding fathers had seen fit to expunge.

A similar effect operates in the domain of psychiatric terminology. Words introduced into the medical lexicon to refer in a scientifically neutral way to certain disturbing mental disorders have a way of picking up unpleasant associations when laypersons start using them. Eventually, this necessitates striking the troublesome terms from the profession's diagnostic manual and substituting new, neutral terms. In the course of a century, the morally insane became psychopaths, and then psychopaths became sociopaths.

Psychiatrists never seem to consider the possibility that their linguistic frustration stems from the inherently disagreeable qualities of sociopaths. Nor do parapsychologists ever seem to consider the possibility that their linguistic frustration stems from the inherently agreeable qualities of the paranormal.

Hence, itemizing parapsychology's blunders only reinforces and clarifies what was said at the beginning: the word *paranormal* is literal nonsense!

How Category 2 Languages the Paranormal

To a certain extent, the militant skeptics follow the parapsychologists along in lockstep, bandying *paranormal* about as though it actually has an intelligible meaning. But their real predilection is for the word *superstition*. They use that locution in the sense of prevalent but false—or at least unjustified, perhaps even irrational—beliefs, usually beliefs that are tinged with fear.

It is strange that persons who tout their position as a scientific one would enter the fray by using a word so emphatically pejorative in its meaning. And if they think they are participating in a rational debate, defining the paranormal from the outset as false belief would appear to beg the question.

But a prior question can be raised as to whether superstition is, properly speaking, a matter of beliefs at all. Many of the popularly enumerated superstitions partake more of the nature of compulsions than they do of beliefs. Knocking on wood, tossing spilled salt over one's shoulder, walking around rather than under a ladder, avoiding rooms on the thirteenth floors of hotels, plucking four-leaf clover, carrying a rabbit's foot, shaking a chimney sweep's hand, shooing away a black cat before it crosses one's path—all these, and many more superstitions, resemble compulsive rituals more than they do beliefs.

Persons who suffer from compulsions tell us that they enact their rituals as a way of forestalling hazily ominous inner stirrings that they fear may otherwise overwhelm them, not as a way of expressing beliefs. In fact, when questioned about it, compulsives actively deny actually believing that stepping on a crack puts Grandma's back in jeopardy. The average person afflicted with a neurotic symptom retains psychological insight, a quality that is conspicuously lacking in the average sigh cop.

The sigh cops' status as social reformers explains their preference for the word *superstition*. By tagging the paranormal as something false and fearful, they can set it apart as something that is fit to be stomped out or held at bay. These are goals that are typical of crusading social activists.

How Category 3 Languages the Paranormal

For their part, those menacingly righteous funda-Christians opt for the word *occult*. They want to intimidate others by stirring up the nightmarish images of skulls, knives, bloody rituals, and the like that are associated with that word in its ordinary usage. Because the word *hidden* is part of its meaning, *occult* also serves to arouse nefarious suspicions, so it is a natural fit to the blustery rhetorical style favored by fundamentalists.

The funda-Christians are particularly fond of the phrase "dabbling in the occult." the word *dabble* has a silly ring to it and conveys a sense of nonseriousness and superficiality. But it is a strange choice for an epithet of mockery in this context. Are the funda-Christians recommending that someone probe seriously and deeply into the paranormal rather than just dabble in it? Not at all; it is not depth of thought, but conformity of thought, that they want to enforce.

And How the Logs Get Jammed

So parapsychologists, sigh cops, and funda-Christians alike fail to make adequate allowance for the diversity of meanings intrinsic to the subject. Because each viewpoint concentrates on so constricted a range of potential meanings—on so literal an interpretation of the specific words they choose to use—the contending parties never really engage one another in the first place. Each tribe of argufiers flounders loudly around in its own muddy puddle of meanings—meanings that are out of tune with those of the others. This is part of the reason why their controversy never goes anywhere. This is how the logs got jammed.

The only way to set this chaotic situation straight is to invite a fourth category of explorers to the discussion table: the playful paranormalists. It will be our job to uphold the entire fabric of words, with similar or related meanings, that is the vocabulary of the alluringly unknown. Playful paranormalists must distinguish among the paranormal's many submeanings without discriminating against any of them.

For the paranormal is not simply an unknown, but an unknown that is already draped seductively in its own distinctive array of emotional trappings. And that, as I have said, is part of the problem. It becomes increasingly difficult to talk about something—much less really come to know about it— when the people dominating the public dialogue are using loaded language, each bringing their particular bias to the considerations at hand.

Should We Simply Create a New Word?

If we're going to be truly playful paranormalists, then we must at least play with the idea of simply creating a new word for that which we are attempting to define.

By definition, the paranormal's unknown sparks certain lofty feelings (wonder, marvel). It confesses to being quite literally nonsensical, a matter that the everyday vocabulary of the paranormal seems to find somewhat funny (hocus-pocus, mumbo jumbo). The paranormal is an unknown that is allied with certain unsettling feelings (eerie, weird, spooky, uncanny) and that, for some, arouses dark suspicions (the hidden quality of the occult). These subsidiary meanings are what lend to an unknown the characteristic flavor and appeal that is its paranormality, so in that sense the paranormal is an unknown that is conceptually inseparable from its appeal. It follows that this same constellation of satellite connotations eventually would accrue to whatever new word would be introduced to pertain in meaning to the subject.

Since the same linguistic fate that befell the parapsychologists' word *paranormal* awaits any similar venture, playful paranormalists will not dither around on the pretext of coining a technical term. Since *paranormal* has become so familiar in ordinary usage, we playful paranormalists figure we might as well stick with it, as long as it be clearly understood that we are using the word as a cipher for a whole panoply of words and meanings.

It is through the mediation of this richer body of meanings that the word *paranormal* manages, despite its defective connotation, to stitch together as its putative denotation an ungainly assortment of popular mysteries or pseudo-mysteries. We must create a new way of talking about all this. And by coupling *paranormal* with the word *play* in the motto "play and the paranormal," we will be adding an essential ingredient back into the mix—one of the very ingredients, in fact, that the parapsychologists mistakenly thought it necessary to eliminate from the recipe.

I say again, it is a whole body of words and meanings—rather than a single word or small group of words taken literally—that establishes the linguistic context within which an unknown can be experienced, verbalized, savored, and consciously appreciated. That is, known. It is only in this context that the "paranormal" will ever cease to be unknown, and be known.

So we "play and the paranormal"-ists cannot rest content until we have given a plausible account of what place each and every one of the auxiliary meanings has in the paranormal.

Looking closely, we can see that at least four nuances, each creating auxiliary meanings, emerge:

- humor
- figurative language
- contrast and negation
- nonsense

What parts are played by these nuances, and how are these notes blended together into the symphony of our understanding of the paranormal?

Let's explore!

Humor and the Paranormal

A review of the scientific and scholarly literature devoted to humor reveals that those who investigate laughter and mirth have suffered under academic taboos parallel to those that have impeded rational inquiry into the paranormal. "How can humor be a serious subject?" and "How can the paranormal be a serious subject?" are similar and related questions.

What is more, the talent of sublime humorists can verge on the paranormal. In my opinion, that inimitable style of comic genius manifested by the great laughter shamans Jonathan Winters and Robin Williams has more plausible a claim to being certified as a genuinely paranormal ability than do the professed gifts of the garden variety psychic. Those two comedians demonstrably have the capacity to conjure up, as if without effort, an endless stream of hilariously mind-bending minidramas and surrealistically funny personages. Why should this be regarded as any the less uncanny or incomprehensible, in short, any the less paranormal, than the ability to read minds?

Charles Addams, Gahan Wilson, and Gary Larson are the grand masters of an eerie style of comic entertainment that borders on the paranormal in substance and in effect. The central concerns of humorists of this mold overlap with those of serious investigators of the paranormal. The three cartoonists are possessed of a sure instinct for the uncanny, and a knack for bringing it forcefully to the attention of others—traits students of the paranormal should ideally share. Larson's piece is even entitled *The Far Side,* a phrase that also aptly encompasses the range of phenomena classified as paranormal.

Puzzles deriving from the concept of personal identity are of central concern to the study of the paranormal, since they are essential in evaluating claims about personal survival of bodily death, or about reincarnation. Many comedies and much humor turns on complications brought about by confounded identity, or by a character's attempts to disguise his or her true identity.

The history of the study of the paranormal is replete with hoaxes, which share their technique of deception with pranks. Hoaxes are sometimes even indistinguishable from practical jokes, which are undeniably a form of humor. Unfortunately, custom still condones laughter in response to stories about the occurrence of paranormal phenomena. It is as though an implicit social norm permits one to dismiss claims about the paranormal with contemptuous laughter.

Like humor, the paranormal is reflexly associated in everyday language with mental illness. Zany, bizarre, hysterical, crazy, madcap, funny farm, *Mad* magazine, cracking up—these and other phrases illustrate that there is a systematic ambiguity in language such that many words are informally applied both to mental illness and to humor. Analogously, many people are quick to label others reporting paranormal experiences as mentally ill, a mistake that a few mental health practitioners still make.

Figurative Language and the Paranormal

Like humor, discourse about the paranormal hinges on an engagingly irregular use of language—a nonliteral use of language—that is meant to bring about an effect that can be consciously appreciated. It is said that humor involves the production of incongruity in the service of mirth. Similarly, discourse about the paranormal alternates solely figurative (that is, nonliteral) meanings with vacuously negative meanings, in order to evince an enticing sense of wonder or an unsettling sense of strangeness.

Figurative language is inalienably implicated in the paranormal, often in the guise of a spatial metaphor that expresses inaccessibility; something that is "far away," out of reach, and unavailable to us regular mortals.

Clairvoyance, for example, is said to be an ability to perceive as if by seeing that which is taking place "out of sight"; but this clearly cannot be referring merely to the kind of spatial displacement for which a telescope or television could correct. And the notion of an afterlife is often cast into words as a spatial metaphor (the world beyond, the other side).

The propensity to enlist spatial concepts in an attempt to capture the distinctive elusiveness of the paranormal in words is rooted in common usage. The word *strange* originally meant that which pertained to a land other than the speaker's own. Because what was foreign could induce wonder and astonishment, those effects were gradually incorporated into the meaning of the word. *Outlandish* evolved along those same lines.

Varying the spatial metaphor can alter the effect. *Occult* bespeaks a paranormal that is out of reach because it is hidden. Since the hiding agent is left unspecified, the meaning of *occult* can preoccupy funda-Christians and other rigid persons with paranoid or obsessional tendencies.

Contrast and Negation and the Paranormal

Notions of proof and evidence are defined within logic, science, and other systems that make use of propositions or statements having literal meanings. There is no conventionally established system that permits proving merely figurative sentences. This is another good reason to be dubious about the claims of parapsychologists. For the paranormal cannot back up its figures of speech with literal equivalents. Instead, it switches to a voice of contrast and negation. Words that are interdefined with the paranormal often are explicitly negative in their meanings (unseen, unknown, unbelievable, uncanny, anomalous, incredible). This quality of being "contrary" to that which "is" is very rare (have you ever seen a thing that is *unseen*, known a thing that is *unknown?*). It is what I call a *contrariety!*

A clash of contrary meanings can galvanize the attention, and many people are readily infatuated with the linguistic interplay of opposites. The ancient Greek Philosopher, Heraclitus the Obscure, made his reputation as a philosopher by exploiting this principle, propounding quandaries such as, "The way up and the way down are one and the same." More recently, we see these kinds of contrarieties all over the place in Neale Donald Walsch's *Conversations with God,* in which it is noted, "in the absence of that which is not, That Which Is, is not," and in which God is described as the great "Am-Not Am."

Discourse about the paranormal pits meaning against meaning, leading the listener along in a manner that satisfies and amuses. This antithetical style helps explain the rebellious streak that seems inherent in the paranormal, and scientists or scholars who take the paranormal seriously, becoming insistent literalists, are outcasts.

The parapsychologists' ongoing effort to storm their way into the halls of science is self-defeating. They make use of a linguistic ruse in an attempt to sneak into science with a subject that is unknown, not just as a matter of fact, but as a matter of definition. For contrariety is part of the essence of the language of the paranormal; hence the oppositional nature of parapsychologists.

The great eighteenth-century skeptical philosopher David Hume imparted an anthropomorphic twist to this contrariety, defining a miracle as "a violation of the laws of nature." Perhaps this is why sigh cops perceive a need to be enforcers.

Nonsense and the Paranormal

Both the unsecured, figurative language of the paranormal and its uninformative contrasts and negations are ways of expressing unavailability, but by endlessly cycling back and forth from one to the other, discourse about the paranormal engenders literal nonsense. That is, to the insistent literalist it will make no sense at all.

The paranormal frankly owns up to its own nonsense by including in its elementary vocabulary a smattering of terms that were dreamed up specifically to serve as nonsense words. *Mumbo jumbo* and *hocus-pocus* were fashioned on the model of the meaningless ritual utterances of sorcerers, magicians, illusionists, and the like.

In the final analysis, the paranormal is inaccessible neither because it is displaced to an unreachable location, nor because there is no scientific explanation for it. Rather, it is inaccessible because it is literally nonsensical. Thus, the paranormal will always remain inaccessible to the insistent literalist. The only "possibility of accessibility" lies in the hands of the playful paranormalist! For the playful paranormalist understands that the literal nonsense that is the paranormal is not just any literal nonsense. It is a characteristically enjoyable nonsense. It amuses, like *Box and Cox*, J. M. Morton's 1847 comedy about two men of those names who, unbeknownst to one another, rented the same room. One tenant was at home only during the night, and the other was there only by day, so neither was aware of the other's existence.

The paranormal's suspenseful allure is verbalized as a Box and Cox drama of reciprocally alternating meanings. The figurative meaning dashes out the back door just as the negative meaning rushes in through the front entrance. The paranormal yields comic relief by bringing its Box and Cox style of linguistic razzle-dazzle to bear on what are at once deep-seated and profoundly anxiety-provoking human concerns—death, the future, and the privacy of a person's innermost thoughts and feelings.

5

BELIEVING THE UNBELIEVABLE BELIEVABLY

So far, so good, for it seems that almost no one is immune to the siren song of the paranormal. Yet why, then, should we intuitively suspect, as so many people do, that interest in the paranormal is something that can be abnormal? Why does taking a strong interest in the subject smack vaguely of mental or emotional disorder? I propose it is because it looks as if we are believing in the unbelievable. And we are. Except when we are not.

How can this be so? Simple. As we have now shown, most of what we know of the paranormal we know not from observed data, but from the words people use to talk about it. Thus, both believing and disbelieving pertain solely to statements, propositions, and so on, that are capable of being either true or false. What we say (and thus, what we think we know) about the paranormal is—as we took great pains to point out in chapter 4—a variety of literal nonsense. And to say of a sentence that it is literal nonsense is, in part, to say that that sentence does not say something that is either true or false. By this argument, therefore, the paranormal can neither be believed nor be disbelieved.

Contrary to a widespread impression, neither paranormal experiences nor interest in the paranormal are symptomatic of psychosis. It is common for schizophrenics, manics, and paranoids to ramble on about the paranormal, to be sure, but it is also common for them to ramble on about politics, religion, celebrities, and scientific matters—rays, vibrations, and such. To understand precisely what kind of psychological abnormality it is that has to do specifically with interest in the paranormal, however, it is necessary first to take stock of how the concept of belief and disbelief becomes entangled in the vocabulary of the alluringly unknown.

The three prevailing theorists—the parapsychologist, the professional skeptic, and the fundamentalist—all being insistent literalists, approach the paranormal as a matter for belief or disbelief. To them it is as simple as that. One either believes in the paranormal or one does not, as though the psychology of believing or disbelieving is all there is to the human psychology of the paranormal.

The sigh cops take pleasure in pointing out that parapsychologists allow themselves to be swayed in their deliberations by beliefs; but sigh cops are blissfully unaware of how easily they themselves succumb to belief in the guise of disbelief. They fail to realize that, in doing so, they are trying to assimilate the paranormal with the same kinds of cognitive capacities as are the parapsychologists. And the funda-Christians are the most uncritical of believers in the paranormal. They believe it exists all right, but that it is not what it appears to be, but rather, is the work of Satan. Theirs is a belief that is modified by their being under the spell of their own favorite, Satan-based pseudo-explanation of not only the paranormal, but just about everything.

All of this is why I am saying that it is time now for the playful paranormalist to enter the discussion. We must sound a strong note of caution here. There are several good reasons for being suspicious of the efforts of the three mainstream parties to magnify believing and disbelieving into being the main focus of any discussion of the paranormal. There is more to our human considerations of the paranormal than whether we believe or disbelieve what we have heard. There is also neither believing nor disbelieving, but simply agreeing to explore it further—agreeably.

It is difficult to do this, however, when, as we at last join the discussion, we find ourselves prey to some mighty persnickety kinds of believing—especially that practiced by the fundamentalists.

The funda-Christians' God seems to require an extraordinary amount of support for His grand design in the form of a lot of very precise believing, and from every one of us, because to a funda-Christian it is extremely important to get one's believing just right. Indeed, before becoming a bona fide, genuine funda-Christian believer, a beginning believer first must appear to be the master of a double Bibleful or more of what may seem to a naive prebeliever to be nothing more than hairsplitting verbal distinctions. Not only that, the funda-Christians would like to conscript all the rest of us, too, into their regimented plan for believing. However, not all of us like to do our believing in a military manner.

One conspicuous feature of belief and disbelief is how quickly and capriciously they can be transformed from one into the other, through the inexplicable process known as conversion. Ideologues have a way of switching sides overnight, converting from one fixed system of beliefs to another, and there is no rational accounting for these instantaneous "awakenings."

Furthermore, excessively vocal, intrusive believing or disbelieving can be just a mental ruse, covering up its opposite number. An inner insecurity of preconscious disbelieving plainly is seething just below the surface of those fundamentalists' minds when, in their familiar, semiaccusatory manner, they demand to know, "Are you a Christian?" (I reply, "Do you mean Jesus or JAY-zus?")There is a deeper puzzle, too, about believing and disbelieving, in their relationship to the paranormal. Strictly speaking, it is not intelligible that the paranormal could be a matter for believing or disbelieving at all. An essential aspect of what one is doing, by saying that one believes a proposition or statement, is to claim that the proposition or statement is true; an essential aspect of what one is doing, by saying that one disbelieves a proposition or statement, is to claim that the proposition or statement is false. In other words, as I said at the top of this chapter, both believing and disbelieving pertain solely to statements, propositions, and so on, that are capable of being either true or false. I repeat what I said earlier. The paranormal is a variety of literal nonsense. What we have said about it does not say something that is either true or false. By this argument, therefore, the paranormal can neither be believed nor disbelieved.

But how can this be? Seemingly adamantly believing and disbelieving paranormalists are a dime a dozen, and they all certainly seem to be believing or disbelieving. They vow, swear and declare they believe or disbelieve, and their tempers may flare if they are challenged in their seeming believing or in their seeming disbelieving. For all of that, the paranormal is something that is not susceptible to being either true or false, hence the paranormal cannot meaningfully be said to be believed or disbelieved.

The seeming believing and seeming disbelieving that grip the fans of the paranormal have a dramatic flair, and therein lies the solution to the puzzle. The theater of belief and disbelief, and their essential interchangability, is part of the continuing drama of the paranormal.

The believers love it when a formerly skeptical person sees the light, and the debunkers welcome reformed parapsychologists into their fold. The funda-Christians rejoice when a believer in the occult turns away from his or her old preoccupations and comes home to JAY-zus. The convert makes the rounds of the talk shows staged by the various televised dramato-funda-Christian organizations.

To a playful paranormalist, all these stock scenarios are further evidence of the gamelike nature of the whole hubbub. The controversy about the paranormal presents a picture of recurrent stylized, stereotyped, and even essentially ceremonialized confrontations, and the three mainstream parties are swallowed up to become part of the drama: they become a moiety of the paranormal.

> We are not talking about believing
> or disbelieving at all,
> but rather, about MAKE-believing

Given that the seeming believing and the seeming disbelieving of the paranormal have a dramaturgic function, it is not really believing and disbelieving at all, but, rather, pseudo-believing and pseudo-disbelieving that propel the controversy about the paranormal. Moreover, lest it be thought that this notion of pseudo-believing and pseudo-disbelieving is being introduced ex post facto merely to discredit the three hidebound frames of reference, playful paranormalism will now proceed to prove that there are such conditions as pseudo-believing and pseudo-disbelieving.

Believing the Unbelievable—Believably

You are about to understand why I titled this chapter as I did. For I am postulating here that it is possible for the human being to believe something and to not believe it at the same time. This is what I call *pseudo-believing*.

Now pseudo-believing must exist if any sense at all is to be made of the nonordinary realm peopled by dyed-in-the-wool fans of professional wrestling—which, by the way, has become one of the highest-rated and most-watched television entertainments of our day.

In many ways, the fans seem to believe, even fervidly to believe, and ringside agitators who voice doubt about the reality of the matches often are threatened with physical assault. (Besides, the fans "see" the wrestlers get hurt).

The fans ogle the gravest villainies that bad guys can perpetrate on good guys. Eye-gouging, jagged metal bottle caps and other deadly objects are smuggled into the ring, openly displayed for all but the referee to see. Championships change hands under the most unjust and unfair of circumstances, and the fans—but never the officials—always witness the bad guys cheating to win. Through the whole show, the fans seem to be whipped up into a frenzy of believing and shouting and jumping and stomping and whooping their belief.

Yet the deciding moment for real belief in the reality of professional wrestling is the one in which the powerful overhead spotlight that beams directly down into the ring is extinguished and, simultaneously, the house lights of the arena are switched on. All at once, the spell is broken and the fans file out to disperse as quickly as though the whole thing had never happened. No groups of concerned eyewitnesses afterwards coalesce to demand that some professional wrestlers' association take corrective action; none of the distressed at ringside think to report the matter to a law enforcement agency.

Nor are the wrestling fans troubled in their seeming believing by the fact that the law seems to understand that it is not possible that any responsible adult truly believe that wrestling is real. Civic clubs, organizations of prominent, reputable business persons, raise money for their communities by sponsoring professional wrestling matches, and no formal complaints are ever filed to the effect that the professional wrestling associations are conspiratorially misleading a gullible public into concluding that wrestling is a real sports event. So, the law provides that the wrestling fans' seeming believing is not really believing, but rather that it is *pseudo-believing,* even though the law does not know it under that name. For their part, the fans of wrestling go right on seeming to believe it, because seeming to believe it is the way they enjoy it. (This is exactly what is going on with television soap-opera fans, incidently. And, for that matter, in most other forms of entertainment. So here, again, we see the connection between entertainment and the paranormal.)

For many fans of the paranormal, "seemingly believing" it is the way they enjoy it, too. But—and here comes the fascinating part—there have to be many other fans of the paranormal who enjoy it by seemingly disbelieving it, for half the fun of it, half the fascination, is the controversy over whether it is "real" or not.

Since literal nonsense is neither true nor false, neither can it really be disbelieving that is at issue in the controversy about the paranormal, because disbelieving something is believing that it is false. By their pseudo-disbelieving, the sigh cops perfect the illusion that there really is such a thing as believing in the paranormal. Because when a skeptic counters a parapsychologist's words by seemingly disbelieving them, an effect is created that it was something literally meaningful that the parapsychologist said. Skeptical pseudo-disbelieving, therefore, is necessary for carrying the controversy about the paranormal on in the manner to which it has become accustomed. The sigh cops covertly collude with the parapsychologists, deflecting attention from a complication that otherwise would be a fatal blow to the prospect of their carrying on with a cherished feud. For were it consciously recognized and openly acknowledged that the paranormal is literal nonsense, no controversy in their traditional mode would be possible.

Stick with me now, because I am about to show you an interesting parallel to all of this that will clarify it further. But first I want to make the point that the basic language of the paranormal cannot be blamed for this sad state of affairs. It voices fair warnings that it isn't believable (incredible, unbelievable), warnings that must be heeded literally, since it is here that the distinctive brand of abnormality that is pertinent to enthusiasm for the paranormal can enter the picture. By the time it has come to a question of believing or disbelieving for a given individual, he or she already has fallen in with the illusion that there is something to the paranormal that, by virtue of its being either true or false, can intelligibly be believed or disbelieved. The crucial error is made at the moment someone plugs into the vocabulary of the alluringly unknown already geared up for believing or disbelieving. Thereafter there is no end to the folly: from that point onwards, the enthusiast, whether parapsychologist, sigh cop, or funda-Christian, just can't seem to get the subject off his or her mind.

So, there is an identifiable condition common to all those assiduously pseudo-believing and assiduously pseudo-disbelieving fanciers of the paranormal. The condition is not a recognized diagnostic entity, but it can tenably be classed as abnormal in that it closely parallels a common, recognized, medical and psychiatric disorder. The propensity to *dysbelieve* that is common to parapsychologists, sigh cops, and funda-Christian demonologists bears many points of resemblance to hypochondriasis.

A Clarifying Parallel

Hypochondriasis is another variety of pseudo-believing. Specifically, it is a condition of seeming belief that one is seriously ill. Hypochondriacs certainly seem to believe that they are ill, and their seeming belief that they are ill will introduce itself into all of their conversations at its earliest convenience. However pertinaciously hypochondriacs may represent themselves as believing that they are sick, it just doesn't make good common sense (nor is it sound epistemology) to maintain that their condition is one of ordinary, straightforward believing that at all.

In fact, a widely accepted clinical understanding of their behavior is that, through their apparent belief that they are ill, hypochondriacs are seeking relationships with their physicians. This clinical explanation is strongly supported by the fact that a highly effective treatment that helps hypochondriacs with their chronic anxiety has been derived from that explanation as a corollary. Elaborating on that treatment plan is obviously beyond the scope of a work about the paranormal, but elucidating how closely hypochondriasis resembles dysbelieving in or about the paranormal brings about some fresh insights into both conditions.

Both hypochondriasis and systematic dysbelieving about the paranormal consist of a mental state of fascinated absorption, the one in certain common and normal physiological sensations, including peristalsis, heartbeats, minor aches and pains, twitches, and twinges, the other in certain common and normal experiences, including apparitions of deceased persons, near-death experiences, deathbed visions, dreams that afterwards unaccountably come true, episodes of seeming unaccountably to know what some other person is thinking, and coincidences that amaze by seeming to come with a personal meaning attached. Hypochondriacs behave as though their own normal, physiological sensations were signs or symptoms of serious illness. Dysbelieving paranormalists behave as though those common and normal (though eerie and wondrous) experiences were an evidential or explanatory basis for intelligible disputation for or against life after death, precognition, telepathy, and so forth. So the perpetrators of both these conditions preoccupy themselves by taking something that is relatively common and normal to be strongly indicative of something else that is relatively extraordinary, whether by being abnormal or by being paranormal.

The pseudo-believing of hypochondriasis and the pseudo-believing and complementary pseudo-disbelieving of the paranormal all are noted for their invincibility to certain ordinary canons or tenets of rational procedure. All those suborders of dysbelievingdom are impregnable to certain usual, standard mechanisms of correction. The hypochondriac's pseudo-believing about being ill is more than a match for the best medical reassurance that the best doctors unanimously can offer on the basis of all the most skilled physical examinations and most sophisticated diagnostic tests, often repeated and uniformly favorable. Nor can any dysbelieving paranormalist be dissuaded from his or her respective seeming believing that scientific verification is just around the corner or already accomplished, or that it is all just perilous hoax, lie, overwishing, neurons on the blink, or that it's the devil trying to lead all of us away from the Lord and straight down to hell. But playful paranormalism has been underscoring all along how inchoate, incorrigible, and unproductive that controversy always has been.

Both hypochondriasis and dysbelieving paranormalisms also bind by becoming a person's predictable favorite subject. Both conditions, when long persisted in, come to seem manneristic. Friends, family, or associates of a perseverant dysbeliever come to see the preoccupation as a feature of the putative believer's or the putative disbeliever's personality. Despite what appears to the outside observer to be an automatism, the way they always can be depended upon to bring up the topic of illness or the topic of the paranormal, neither hypochondriacs nor habitués of the various dysbelievings about the paranormal seem to be fully aware of how peculiar their preoccupations can seem to an ordinary person.

In a word, excessive dysbelievers about the paranormal are eccentrics, and it is their eccentricity that is felt as the differentiative abnormality to which over-involved paranormalists are heir. A condition normally is adjudged abnormal partly on the basis of its adverse consequences upon the person who has the condition or upon others in the vicinity. It is a simple matter to trace out some of the importune sequela of dysbelieving paranormalisms.

All their ardent dysbelieving, pro or con, lands paranor-maliacs in some sticky complications—some amusing, others not so funny. The most comical one is that dwelling on the paranormal by seeming to believe it or to disbelieve it can make it seem that the paranormal's meaning is antithetical to the meaning of faith. This rankles certain ill-natured infallibilites—you know who I mean. And for persons of similar persuasion, this may not be the "last laugh," but it is certainly the last straw.

Faith Enters the Picture

Faith has not just one meaning, but a gamut of them. It is another word whose meaning has been on the move for a long time. Faith begins simply enough as belief that is not grounded in rational proof or material evidence, and it may confine its meaning there. In other instances, though, it esca-lates to a meaning of unjustified, uncritical, unquestioning, unswerving belief. It may crystallize into a system of adamant-ly and inflexibly held beliefs, and it may define itself as one particular religion. From there, faith has been known to rev its meaning all the way up to what should be believed, according to that particular believer, or to what must be believed, or had better be believed, according to its particular authority, or else.

The funda-Christians, and all their fellow fundamental-ists, set up their camps of meaning in that latter quadrant, out in the harsh wastelands of faith's spread of meanings. It is only out there in their desert, and under the condition that the para-normal is held to be something that can be or ought to be either believed or disbelieved, that the paranormal could be imagined to come into conflict with faith.

A less edictful person would be as impressed by similari-ties in meaning between the words *faith* and *paranormal* as by their differences. Faith and the paranormal coincide, for instance, in their being unsupported, as believing, by rational proof or by evidence. Faith and the paranormal do vary some-what in their reactions to that circumstance, however. As a believing, the paranormal sometimes worries that it has never been proven. It hopes to get backed up by proof or evidence, or at least parapsychologists like to say that it does. Faith, though, is a believing that boasts that it is proud of its unprovenness. Still, and as strangely as we would expect, faith does sometimes forget itself by seeming to be happy to hear, for example, that an American astronaut who overflew Mount Ararat spotted some pieces of Noah's Ark down there. And many a bumbling proponent of "creation science" (a funda-Christian rationalization for the existence of fossils and such) has argued that marks in Cretaceous limestone in the bed of the Paluxy River in Texas prove that humans and dinosaurs roamed the earth at the same time, and hence that conventional scientists' time-scales of evolution are all wrong.

And neither can "faith" be completely distinguished in meaning from nonsense. Anyone earnestly inquiring into the meaning of faith will be led swiftly, and as a matter of logical necessity, into the adjacent linguistic and conceptual territory of nonsense. The early Christian theologian Tertullian (160–230 A.D.) declared that his faith "is to be believed because it is absurd." Since then, a number of Christian thinkers, but probably no funda-Christian ones, have understood why the issue of the proximity of faith to nonsense is logically an unavoidable one. The very best of us paranormalists also wish we could get the public to realize that the paranormal is logically, literally, and linguistically nonsensical, just as so much humor is.

6

KNOWING THE UNKNOWABLE

Everyone is interested in the paranormal. Even those who say they are not interested show their interest by the vividness of their declarations of noninterest. And now, at the turn of the century, we are seeing a peaking of this universal interest in the universe. It has reached a fever pitch. We've all got the fever; a vague sense of dis-ease about things we wish we knew more about. I call this dis-ease *paranormalismosis*.

By pursuing the paranormal's meanings from humor, through figurative language, into the paranormal's contrasts and negations, and thence into its quintessential nonsense, playful paranormalism was able to identify one common, major *abnormality* of the paranormal in the three most virulent strains of dysbelieving *paranormalismosis*. It is through their urgent dysbelievings that the insistent literalists who are the three regular players, the members of the drama's standard cast of characters, manage to conceal from everyone's conscious attention that, in part, the paranormal is defined as un-knowledge.

With *The Last Laugh*, playful paranormalism has bounced right back to the notion of knowledge and its bearing on the paranormal—right back, that is, to the unknown that is a flagship meaning of the paranormal. What is the nature of this unknown that is at the heart of the paranormal, and how is it set within the context of all the paranormal's attendant meanings?

The unknown that is peculiarly the paranormal's is a decidedly odd kind of unknown. Part of the uncanny feeling felt when contemplating the paranormal is the sense that new knowledge is all set to emerge from it. The paranormal is an unknown that always feels as though it is on the verge of becoming known.

On hearing about near-death experiences, apparitional visits on the part of the departed, veracious premonitions, and the like, one gets a feeling that something profound and surprising is just about to be revealed. The paranormal tantalizes precisely because it presents itself not as the *unknown,* but as a *knowing* that is barely out of reach. It is just around the corner or over the horizon, its wondrous new knowledge is right at hand and soon will be had.

From amidst a mist of all its eerie feelings, the paranormal always seems ready, almost at any moment, to disclose something wondrous and unbelievable. Since this promised new knowledge almost never materializes, the paranormal, like other good entertainment, always leaves them wanting more.

How is it possible that there would be, or seem to be, a variant "unknown" of this same kind? The parallelism between hypochondriasis and dysbelieving paranormalism yields a clue to the answer.

Hypochondriasis shares a remarkable peculiarity with only a handful of other medical conditions: To be a hypochondriac, a person must have a prior existing concept of illness. That is, hypochondriasis is a meta-illness (if I may coin a term). It is an illness that is *about* illness.

If someone had no idea what illness is, it would not confer on them any immunity from tuberculosis, coryza, cancer, rabies, bleeding ulcer, cellulitis, osteoporosis, plague, myasthenia gravis, measles, mumps, lupus, tularemia, or any other illness. But a human being first must be injected with the germ of a concept of illness in order for a case of hypochondriasis to develop.

Is the peculiarity of the paranormal parallel to the peculiarity of hypochondriasis? Is the paranormal linguistically and logically parasitic on some other, prior, ordinary concept as hypochondriasis is linguistically and logically parasitic on the prior, ordinary concept of illness? If so, what could that other, prior, ordinary concept be?

Playful paranormalism posits that the paranormal is parasitic on the prior, ordinary concept of *knowledge*.

That is, we must know there is a thing called "knowledge" before we can conceive of a thing that stands outside of that knowledge as that which cannot be "known."

And playful paranormalism surmises that the strangeness of the paranormal's "unknown" somehow resides in its presupposing a prior concept of knowledge. That is, unless I am misbelieving, the paranormal is neither the perhaps-someday soon-to-be-proven, unknown superknowing of parapsychologists, nor the preepistemic protoknowing of sigh cop lore, nor the devilish deceptoknowing of demonizing funda-Christians. Rather, the paranormal is a secondary elaboration upon a precedent notion of long and firmly established knowledge.

This preexistent knowledge is needed as a backdrop against which a phenomenon can, by virtue of its own seeming contrariness toward that preexistent knowledge, be made to seem unknown in that wonderful way that so appeals to all of us paranormalists.

So it is only on the solid ground of knowledge that death is such a final sort of thing, and that Uncle Hamperd has been dead for years, that it can seem "paranormal" for Aunt Florene to have seen him in the parlor one night last week.

Playful paranormalism submits that there must be a background of prelusive knowledge for a phenomenon to seem paranormal. That is, a phenomenon's seeming "paranormality" entails that it seem contrary to something that already has been very long and very well known.

Using the "vocabulary of the paranormal," which we discussed at length in an earlier chapter (words like *unseen, unbelievable, incredible*) allows us to step away from the vocabulary of that which is already known (what is known is "seen," "believable," "credible"). Thus, our description of these paranormal events is not limited by having to use words that cannot describe them.

Invoking the vocabulary of the alluringly unknown sets aside a linguistic protectorate within a context of prelusive knowledge in which it is permissible (although admittedly eerie, wondrous, bizarre, anomalous, or weird) to say that a dead grandma came back home for a visit, that a fortune-teller foretold a tornado, or that a psychic can read someone's mind.

A phenomenon's contrariness toward its own prelusive knowledge (the fact that it produces an effect opposite to everything we knew ahead of time about it) makes that prelusive knowledge seem strangely unfamiliar, and that is what is needed for that phenomenon to seem paranormally unknown.

In short, the eerily wondrous effects of the paranormal are the epistemological equivalent of *jamais vu*—that feeling a person has when a situation or condition with which he or she is already very familiar, and fully acknowledges being so, suddenly and unaccountably seems markedly and strangely unfamiliar. And the knowledge that a paranormal phenomenon renders oddly unfamiliar is the prelusive knowledge about that same phenomenon. All the other meanings of the vocabulary of the alluringly unknown are what can tie a phenomenon into a context of prelusive knowledge so that that phenomenon can be made to seem unknown in the manner that we eager fans of the paranormal love and crave and seek.

Playful paranormalism waded into the notion of the paranormal at its leisure, instead of plunging in all at once as the three dysbelieving insistent literalists do, diving right into the paranormal with their notions of belief or disbelief, notions that bring their own attendant concepts of "true" or "false" along with them.

The Journey into Words That Form Our Experience

Playful paranormalism has made a new kind of sense of the paranormal, by first following the conceptual connections of the paranormal as they led to the enjoyment that the paranormal brings by its very nature, and then on through, into epistemology.

This process discloses a major point at which *hyperdysbelieving* about the paranormal diverges markedly from hypochondriasis. Hypochondriacs always are hurrying to their doctors' offices, but hyperdysbelievers about the paranormal always are putting off badly needed visits to see their epistemologists.

The clear implication of playful paranormalism's multidimensional definition is that the paranormal is an eerie experience with an undercoating of pop epistemology and that, accordingly, the vocabulary of the alluringly unknown is a way of entertaining with the concept of knowledge. That is sufficient to show that any overall theory of the paranormal must include an analysis of the language of the subject, whether the theory sets out its analysis explicitly or only presupposes it tacitly or without forethought.

Bad News for Fans of the Paranormal

By now I would guess that the great majority of "fans of the paranormal" are sure to be bored by these lengthy dissertations on the meanings of the paranormal, especially if playful paranormalist theory is correct on its next point: the intricacies of the ordinary vocabulary of the alluringly unknown promote the paranormal's longevity as a familiar variety of popular entertainment.

The ordinary vocabulary of the alluringly unknown descends as a turbid curtain of meanings, obscuring the fact that the paranormal is a diversion. Few audience members ever get curious enough to part that curtain, step backstage, and discern how paranormal entertainment is made.

Many proparanormalists are put off by the suggestion that the paranormal is a culturally transmitted amusement. Oddly, those fans apparently enjoy their paranormal best when it is served on a plate of seeming sensibility, or taken with a buffer of seriousness. For the fans of those wrestling with ideas, just as for the fans of those wrestling with bodies, there must be a modicum of formality such as dysbelieving provides. We can't make fun of this stuff, or the illusion is broken.

Still, those fans' average level of seriousness for their subject must never be so high that they inquire at great depth. Gaining the insight that the paranormal is entertainment and humor would threaten to spoil the fun they take in their kinds of seriousness about it, or so I gather most serious fans of the paranormal would believe. This playful paranormalist assumes, therefore, that the mesmerizing mistiness of the vocabulary of the alluringly unknown favors the long-term survivability of the paranormal as a diversion. I am further assuming that the vocabulary of the alluringly unknown is effective in preserving what is an open secret: that the paranormal is popular entertainment, and that for this reason there may be some or many fans who keep on coming to the show who wouldn't, were it to be advertised as one.

It is as if there was the widespread presumption that openly to recognize the paranormal as the species of entertainment that it is would be to take all the fun out of it, and drive its audience away. On behalf of playful paranormalism, incidentally, I take strong exception to that assumption, since in actuality fun, play, and humor easily weather the conscious realization that the paranormal is entertainment. Truly diligent investigators can go on from there to apply that insight to enhance the amusement that is to be had from the paranormal.

But for now all I want to argue is that, as flimsy a veil as it may be epistemologically, the ordinary vocabulary of the alluringly unknown's dry complexity tends to maintain the fans' average seriousness about the subject at a level that shields them from what, to many, would be, at least initially, a grave disappointment in learning that the paranormal is popular entertainment.

The beguiling power that draws most folks' curiosity to the paranormal in the first place holds it there by providing it with lots of pleasant sensations of mystery, tasty spices for the inner life of cognition. To the average fan, traipsing through a mental obstacle course of distinctions that are interlinked in a complicated, multilevel arrangement probably would seem dull, no fun at all compared to dawdling around in the pleasures of paranormal mysticality.

Whose curiosity wouldn't prefer hanging out in the actual realm of the paranormal, rather than slaving away over a mazy tangle of nuances in meaning? Let's face it, carefully thinking a pathway through a latticework of common language synonyms and near-synonyms that are interaligned in meaning along the fine lines of several levels of distinctions is not just anyone's idea of having a good time. Nevertheless, it happens that the paranormal catches and holds the attention precisely because it itself is just such a latticework of interaligned meanings as they are commonly used to talk about such things as near-death experiences, dreams that come true, mind reading, and ghosts.

I Insist on Insisting

Enough is enough, you say. But in the past no one has ever insisted loudly enough or long enough that, to make sense of the paranormal, it is necessary to buckle down and get at the very words of the subject, and at their meanings. I am going to insist loudly here, because no one that I know of has ever tried to turn the argument around to the matter of the paranormal's loose-jointed hodgepodge of nomenclature, and to question why it is wrought with so many delighted expressions of eerie wondrousness.

Since the paranormal always trades on its curious recreational language, inquiring paranormalists who steer clear of issues of meaning stand convicted of laziness or of cowardice, or of both. And their avoidance of those issues always comes back to haunt them, typically in the form of what I have termed *dysbelieving*.

Words, Names, and Beings: Is Santa Paranormal?

By leafing through the back pages of the paranormal's phrase book, lots more words can be found that bespeak its entertaining power. There are a number of less familiar expressions, more or less synonymous with the ones already included in the basic word list, that evidence the same principles of paranormal meaning that previously were set out.

Mirific, for example, is a jocular term that means "working wonders; marvelous; inducing wonder." And *mirabilia* is synonymous with *wonders, marvels,* or *miracles.* The word *ferly* refers to something wondrous and strange, but with the implication that it excites dread or that it is frightful. These expressions further document the principle that the vocabulary of the alluringly unknown is an admixture of phrases having to do with humor, uplifting wonder, and fear, as well as with what is outside the known or the familiar.

Beyond that, there is a sort of second-order vocabulary of the alluringly unknown, a collection of words that take the basic meaning of *paranormal* as a given and then go on to build on it. They include the names of various paranormal entities—ghosts, banshees, spirit guides, demons—and the names of various paranormal powers such as telepathy, clairvoyance, metagnomy, and telekinesis.

The paranormal's playfulness penetrates into the second-order vocabulary of the alluringly unknown, too. Named paranormal entities slide by degrees into named playbeings. Ghost, spirit guide, demon, fairy, the Tooth Fairy, Santa Claus: it is pointless to try to specify exactly where, in that series, the paranormal ends and play begins.

My native intuition tells me that the great majority of twentieth-century adults would group fairies with Santa. Fairies belong in Peter Pan plays and childrens' fiction. The paranormal is full of surprises, however. Neither education nor intelligence is a reliable gauge of how far people will go before calling it quits, paranormally, and giving themselves over to fun.

Arthur Conan Doyle, a medical doctor who wrote Sherlock Holmes mysteries when he wasn't investigating paranormal ones, took fairies seriously. He wholeheartedly believed a couple of mischievous little girls who produced photographs of the tiny winged people they claimed to have spotted.

A much greater number of people would put demons in with the paranormal, but here, too, the battle lines are drawn across the playing fields. An old naming convention lists stock epithets for athletic teams—the Dogs, the Bulls, the Eagles, the Rangers, the Knights, the Devils, the Sox. Many funda-Christians have concluded that JAY-zus is desperately in need of their assistance in this important matter. Several times lately, fundamentalists have organized to save others' souls by compelling local school boards to rename teams tagged "the Devils" or "the Demons."

Since God is such a weakling that even a high school committee is able to thwart His purposes by bestowing a name on a small-town football team, it is no wonder that the paranormal's very own holiday has Him stymied. He hasn't been able to prevent Satan from deluding Americans into the grave mistake of dressing as demons or witches on Halloween. So God and JAY-zus must be beside themselves with worry that the funda-Christians might fail in their campaign to banish jack-o'-lanterns and trick or treat from public schools.

Meanwhile, the devil is as happy as he can be, counting up the excess souls he expects will be arriving at hell's gate, still wearing their Halloween costumes.

There are very few who would count Santa as a paranormal being. The personification of toy making and of the Christmas spirit of gift giving originated as Saint Nicholas, though, to whom paranormal powers once were attributed. And funda-Christians beware; Santa was accompanied by a demonic assistant, Black Pete, in nineteenth-century iconography.

Is The X-Files *Misleading?*

Nonstandard language also bears out playful paranormalism. Two current items—one of journalistic jargon and one of American slang—are added reminders of how thin the line is between the stage and the supernatural.

A reporter sent out to cover a paranormal phenomenon may call the assignment a "Scully." Dana Scully is a fictional character—a medical doctor who investigates unsolved cases of allegedly supernatural occurrences in a popular Fox Network television series, *The X-Files*. The staff of the *Skeptical Inquirer* thinks the show is a serious threat to the public. A recent issue highlighted *The X-Files* on its cover, and the accompanying article remonstrated against the program's screenwriters for fostering several scientific mistakes on a gullible public. So even "skeptical" dysbelieving minds can get pretty foggy about the nature of fiction at times.

Present-day American fans may humorously refer to a seemingly paranormal occurrence or experience as a "woo-woo." the term is onomatopoeic, a jocular imitation of the sound people may emit involuntarily upon being amazed by something eerily wondrous. This topical expression points up another similarity between humor and the paranormal: Humor also prompts its own characteristic, involuntary vocalization—laughter.

There are other words that clearly do not now qualify to be included in the vocabulary of the alluringly unknown, but that betray by their etymology that they once dabbled in the occult. Someone who is aghast may be experiencing the same or a similar kind of fright or dread that a superstitious person does, or that someone who finds something spooky does. But the word *aghast* presently does not convey the concept of paranormality. Etymologically, though, *ghast* meant *ghost*, and to say that someone was aghast was to say that that person was disturbed by a ghost.

Similarly, *amusement* now is used with no hint of paranormality, but in its origins it alluded to supernatural entities, the Muses. Bemusement is a state of being utterly muddled, or of being confused or bewildered, or in a dream-like reverie, lost in thought, preoccupied. Not only does the paranormal amuse, it also bemuses. So, to quantify it, the fun of the paranormal equals amusement plus bemusement.

There is another class of words that back up playful paranormalism's insight by having some meanings that convey the idea that something is paranormal and other meanings that convey the idea that something is pleasingly appealing. Typically, in any given case in which a word of this class is used, it is clear whether something paranormal is being meant or not.

Charm, for example, may be used to refer to an object with a supernatural power of attracting good or deflecting evil, and in another sense the same word refers to a certain kind of delightful appealingness. Others in this category are: *haunting, enchanting, ensorcelling,* and *magical.*

Then, there are the gray areas of paranormal meaning. There are the categories of expressions for which it often is unclear, even in a single context of their regular usage, whether something paranormal is being meant or not. They are good weasel words, in that a speaker who uses them can, if challenged, back off by saying, for example, "Well, I didn't really mean to be saying anything spooky."

A cluster of expressions interdefined with omen can serve to exemplify these wishy-washy ways. Paranormally speaking, omens are supernatural signs, preternatural portents of good or evil. Omen exists in a verb form, too, one of a family of synonyms that includes prefigure, presage, betoken, portend, adumbrate, odumbrate, prognosticate, forebode, foreshadow, auspicate, and augur.

Over the years, there has been a lot of slippage in the meaning of such terms. Although some of them had their origins in the paranormal, today they are as likely to be used by statisticians as they are by soothsayers.

Foreshadow is also one of a concatenation of words that express the concept of paranormality by association with shadows. Because they seem mysterious, and because they are thought of as immaterial or insubstantial, fleeting or flimsy, shadows make a good metaphor for the paranormal.

The ghosts or spirits of the dead are called *shadows,* and sciomancers divined by means of shadows, or by means of communication with ghosts. *Sciosophy* is a debunkers' term for astrology, palmistry, and other traditional systems of supposedly supernatural knowledge.

For much the same reasons that they have been favored by paranormalists, shadows have had a long and distinguished history in the world of play and entertainment. They are an enduring theme of works of fantasy and are a reliable source of amusement, as in the childhood game of making hand shadows. Shadow plays once thrived in India and still are popular in Bali.

The concept of serendipity also is situated somewhere in the shadowlands of semiparanormal meaning. Serendipity is an assumed aptitude for making valuable or desirable discoveries by accident or in the process of looking for something else. Is that type of gift paranormal or not?

On the plus side, serendipity, like the paranormal, is intrinsically negative in its meaning: something is found that is not sought for. Most dictionaries note that serendipity is a "supposed" or "assumed" talent, just as they do when defining alleged paranormal abilities such as telepathy or precognition.

Like the paranormal, the notion of serendipity is deep-rooted in popular entertainment. Horace Walpole (1717–1797) extracted the concept and the name from an amusing Persian fairy tale about three princes of Serendip (Sri Lanka). By the dictionary's definition, all of serendipity's discoveries are happily profitable ones; serendipity is comic in spirit, like most of the paranormal.

In Walpole's words, serendipity is a faculty the three princes exemplified for "making discoveries, by accidents and sagacity, of things they were not in quest of." So serendipity resembles the paranormal in that it also entails a prior concept of knowledge (sagacity).

Over in the minus column, serendipity and the paranormal disagree in how they handle their own prior knowledge. Paranormal entertainment is played on a stage of common knowledge, but it is played so smoothly that most folks never notice the platform of preestablished knowledge standing there. The vocabulary of the alluringly unknown, like a good actor in a good drama, makes the stage seem to disappear. For a while, a paranormalizing person forgets about the old, established knowledge being there at all.

Serendipity has an entirely different relationship in consciousness to its own background knowledge than the paranormal does to its own. During an episode of serendipity, someone marvels in a new, personal revelation as knowledge already possessed suddenly illuminates a perceived chance occurrence. Serendipitizing persons consciously are appreciating their own operative background knowledge as they make novel discoveries; that is their sagacity.

Serendipity highlights its prior knowledge. It brings what it already knows to the fore to yield a fortunate discovery. As Walpole defined it, serendipity is a concept that echoes Pasteur's observation that chance favors the prepared mind.

There are lots of discoveries about the paranormal that are waiting to be made in the dictionary. The observations of generations of paranormal watchers are lying dormant in language. Numerous rare, outdated, obsolete, or archaic words are potential sources of studies that can add to contemporary understanding of the paranormal.

There is no better illustration of this principle than the old word *fey*. Not only does it name a common, seemingly paranormal phenomenon that present-day investigators have passed over, but it also is a word of wide-ranging paranormal meaning. *Fey* commingles many of the standard meanings of the vocabulary of the alluringly unknown, and then it adds a striking observation of its own. It describes an unrecognized paranormal phenomenon that frequently occurs among those who are about to die. This extraordinary phenomenon can be readily confirmed by physicians, nurses, or hospice workers who study peri-mortal experiences.

Fey is a good linking word; it brings together many of the specific component meanings of the paranormal that already have been identified. In one of its several senses, it is a simple synonym of paranormal, since it can mean *supernatural, otherworldly,* or *strange. Fey* also is related in meaning to humor (it sometimes means whimsical) and to fear (it can refer to a state of apprehension of impending death or other calamity.) *Fey* also brings the abnormal fringe of paranormal consciousness into play, because it can mean "disordered in mind," "mad," "touched in the head," "out of one's mind," or "markedly disturbed by fear of approaching death." *Fey* can refer to a paranormal ability to see the future and is sometimes synonymous with *clairvoyant.* Since *fey* also means "the ability to see fairies," it can be a second-order expression of the vocabulary of the alluringly unknown that makes reference to a type of paranormal entity. *Fey* even has a meaning that will please those obtrusive old crosspatches, the funda-Christians. In years gone by, *fey* also meant "accursed."

There is another meaning of *fey* that is more significant for the study of the paranormal than any of those above, however. It can denote strange, exultant behavior that often immediately precedes death, a state of unnaturally high spirits or elation that frequently can be observed among persons just before they pass away. When contemporary lexicographers define this sense of *fey,* they tend to specify that it is a "supposed" state of consciousness that was "formerly believed" immediately to precede death. Expressions like those signal that modern folks don't recognize fey as an actual phenomenon. Today's dictionary makers assume that the old idea that the dying become fey is just an old wives' tale.

From personal experience at the bedsides of the dying, however, I know that the phenomenon exists and is fairly common. I suspect that the reason the average person is not aware of it anymore is that, earlier in the twentieth century, the locale of dying was shifted from the home to hospitals. Doctors and nurses gently ushered the loved ones of dying patients out of the room prior to the terminal event. Medical personnel believed that witnessing death would devastate family members emotionally. Fey was forgotten by the community at large as a consequence of these medical practices.

Standards of care of the dying are changing again, and family members now are being encouraged to remain with their loved ones until the very end. Doctors and nurses often make themselves scarce at that point, so families can experience those amazing closing moments of life together. So I suspect that the general public soon will become aware of that strange state of consciousness again.

Single Words or Phrases Aren't the Only Culprits

Playful paranormalists who study the ordinary language of the paranormal shouldn't concentrate only on single words or short phrases. The accepted modes of everyday discourse about the supernatural also encompass several lengthier units of language. They take the form of common qualifier clauses, the standard disclaimers that customarily are dropped so unobtrusively into narrations about paranormal phenomena that they hardly are noticed at all.

"I never believed in that sort of thing before, but . . ."
"I always thought that people who were interested in the paranormal were crazy, but . . ."
"No one in my family ever took ghosts or ESP seriously, but . . ."
"I had been a skeptic all my life, but . . ."

These and an array of equivalent locutions are sprinkled liberally throughout the corpus of firsthand accounts of paranormal experiences. Usually, when someone describing a seemingly paranormal phenomenon introduces one of these stock formulas, the conversation flows right on along without so much as a ripple.

But to a playful paranormalist's trained ear that "but" sounds fishy. He interrupts at that point to ask why such formulations are prevalent in accounts of paranormal phenomena.

They are cliche's casually and cleverly planted there to butter up the listener or reader. Ostensibly, they establish that the speaker or writer is a reasonable person; perversely, they serve to soften up the audience's critical faculties. These tag lines crop up so frequently that playful paranormalists count them as one of the distinguishing features of narratives concerning paranormal phenomena.

The Connection with Entertainment Is Established

On this long safari through the backwaters of paranormal meaning we have bagged quite a few more specimens that help establish the close kinship between the paranormal and entertainment. It is one more indicator of how lax the dysbelievers have been about the core meanings of a field that is far more dependent on words than are most disciplines.

To reemphasize: as tedious and uninteresting as it is, this way of proceeding is *not* pedantry. The dullness, dryness, boringness, and seeming irrelevance of precise questions of meaning help explain why the fact that the paranormal is entertainment has gone unnoticed for so long. Dysbelievers are enmazed in the labyrinthine architecture of the basic language of the paranormal. Unnodding attentiveness to words and meanings is a thread of Ariadne that scholarly playful paranormalists can follow to find startling new ways of knowing about the unknown.

In order for the vocabulary of the alluringly unknown to be used to entertain, it must coact with a substructure of established knowledge. How is the paranormal's recreational language related to its titillative epistemology? To answer that, it helps to place the paranormal into the specific category of amusements and diversions to which it belongs.

7

CLASSIFYING THE PARANORMAL

So far in our journey we have taken a close look at what have been, until now, the three categories of legitimate discussers of the paranormal, and the reasons for opening the logjam they have created by inviting a fourth category—playful paranormalist—to the table. We've also explored a new way of looking at the paranormal itself, seeing its playful or entertaining side, and thus legitimizing the role of the playful paranormalist in the discussion. Finally, we've examined the role that believing and "dysbelieving," and the vocabulary of the paranormal have played in creating our attitudes and shaping our understandings (or perhaps our misunderstandings) around this topic.

Now let's take a closer look at the paranormal itself, see if we can't come closer to understanding what it is and what it is not, and maybe even see some similarities between it and other of our life experiences and activities—similarities that may help us recognize (to "know again") what we are looking at.

Playful paranormalism's definitive statement about what the paranormal is—namely, entertainment; a diversion—smooths the way for an elegant and warrantable classification.

Definition and classification are distinct but collateral activities, so it confounds playful paranormalist that practitioners of the three major dysbelievings pay so little attention to the consequential problem of how the paranormal is to be classified.

The insight that the paranormal is tightly connected to entertainment and fun makes it possible to place the paranormal in a class with other pastimes or entertainments that also are pursued for the same reason that the paranormal is pursued: because they alter consciousness in ways that are perceived as desirable. These diversions overlap with the paranormal in other significant respects, including the fact that they are interrelated with humor, and are undergirded by prior conceptions of knowledge. That is, there are things we think we know about them, yet the experience of the pastimes themselves often leads us to conclusions opposite to that which we think we know.

I have called this class of pastimes the *periparanormal*. To participate in any one of these pastimes is to frolic along the fun-filled frontiers between the known and the unknown. The periparanormal delights by cooking up a felt state of dynamic tension between knowledge and nescience. Each component divertissement accomplishes this in its own uniquely entertaining fashion. The paranormal does precisely the same thing, by setting itself against a background of sound knowledge, long known, with which it seems to be in sharp disagreement.

Let's take a look at some categories of what I am calling the periparanormal, and see if you can see the parallels that I see, and what this might tell both of us about this entire topic.

A: Gambling

Gambling fits neatly within this category. It comes as a shock to hear gambling classified with entertainment, partly because it sometimes has adverse effects on those who overindulge in it, partly because the prospect of getting something for nothing affronts our Puritan side. Nonetheless, people who are gambling certainly appear to be amusing themselves. In order to gamble, they flock to resorts where stage shows and other lavish entertainments are also available. Randomizing apparatus that could as easily have been used in a gaming establishment was found in the ruins of an ancient Greek oracle, where it had been used for fortune-telling. Some archaeologists hold that dice originated as divination devices and that their use in games of chance was a later development. They are also used in many board games.

Gamblers dote on luck, a concept that, like omen words, can't quite make up its mind whether it wants to be paranormal or not. Like the paranormal, luck lends itself to figures of speech. For example, gamblers personify chance as Lady Luck. The concepts of luck and the paranormal intersect in certain archetypal symbols of superstition—horseshoes and other good luck charms. Many gamblers rely on talismans to bring them good fortune. The ever-versatile *fey* sometimes means "unlucky," and *serendipity* sometimes is used loosely to mean "good luck."

Extraordinary coincidences that seem to be personally meaningful are attributed by some paranormalists to the operation of synchronicity; it may seem to a person experiencing that type of coincidence that something inexplicably magical has just occurred. Gamblers often are overcome by an uncanny conviction that they are just about to win; more rarely, that conviction appears to be fulfilled, giving an impression of magical foreknowledge. So the psychology of chance that enchants gamblers is similar to that found among paranormalists. Habitual gamblers are notoriously superstitious. The same charge is customarily directed against us proponents of the paranormal.

B: Recreational Drug Use

So-called recreational drug use also overlaps with both the paranormal and entertainment. The history of nitrous oxide (laughing gas) is a prime example. Today, this substance is popular among physicians as an anesthetic agent, but before that use was discovered, it was employed to induce mystical consciousness, and even enjoyed a vogue as a public entertainment. William James and other philosophers, scientists, and psychologists inhaled nitrous oxide as a means of achieving metaphysical insights or of discerning alternate realities. Benjamin Blood extolled the state induced by the drug by speculating that "the atmosphere of the highest of all possible heavens must be composed of this Gas." By early in the nineteenth century, laughing gas was being used for theatrical purposes. In 1814 the American journalist Moses Thomas wrote about his visit to a kind of theater of consciousness in Philadelphia, where the proprietor dispensed laughing gas for the education and amusement of his audience.

C: Wide-Eyed Wonderment

This was in the same fine tradition as the institutions created over a century later by another great American periparanormalist, Robert Ripley. For decades, Ripley traveled the world and pored over countless books in search of the curiosities he reported in his wildly popular newspaper cartoon *Believe It or Not*. He collected incredible coincidences, developmental anomalies, extraordinary happenings, stories of persons with incredible talents, bizarre facts, and other kinds of odd and unusual information and presented them in a way that astounded and entertained his readers. His finds include a man who could infallibly determine the sex of the person who had written any given sample of handwriting by means of a key hanging from a silk thread; two unrelated sets of twin girls both named Lorraine and Loretta Szymanski, who turned up in the same classroom and whose families were found to be living just a few doors from each other; and a woman in Massachusetts who discovered, several weeks after giving birth, that perfect likenesses of her infant had suddenly and unaccountably appeared on her knees (supported with impressive photographic evidence).

Ripley's cartoons challenged fans at home to send in items of startling and offbeat information. At the height of the craze, letters poured into his office by the thousands, and he selected the best contributions for publication. Many of the artifacts he accumulated and much of the knowledge he acquired were subsequently assembled and displayed in his Odditoriums, later known as the various Ripley's Believe It or Not Museums. The effects of Ripley's work upon consciousness approximate those of purportedly paranormal experiences and phenomena.

D: Bemused Reporting

The professional subspecialty constituted by journalists who collect and disseminate what they term "weird news" can also be subsumed under the periparanormal. They gather offbeat information from legitimate news sources only (never the tabloids), classify it, then publish it. One standard category appearing in these collections is that of news stories, corroborated by journalistic means, though not necessarily by scientific or scholarly means, that have to do with the supernatural. A recent compendium includes, for example, tales of a woman who was struck by lightning while reading a Stephen King novel that pictured a man being struck by lightning on its cover; a phantom airplane crash at the end of a residential street in Pennsylvania seen, heard, and smelled by witnesses, but with no wreckage being found; a rash of spectral clown sightings in St. Paul; and a panoply of appearances by the real Virgin Mary. Specialists in weird news marshal the items they accumulate in such a way as to astonish and to amuse their readers. The books that result from their efforts are of equal interest to devotees of humor and of the paranormal.

E: Travel—Real and Fantasy

Certain prodigies of tourism belong in the family of periparanormal pastimes, too. They include not only travel to those places that are the common destinations of the psychically curious—famous haunted houses, ancient pyramids, and all the other locations with reputations for paranormality—but especially the travels, writings, and biographies of those peregrinating, eccentric adventurers whose names crop up so regularly in the history of the paranormal. Those intrepid souls who forswore familiar comfort and convenience to venture into distant, unknown reaches took up travel in large part for the way it could alter awareness. They sought exotic spectacles in faraway lands for the sheer thrill of novelty and discovery. Often, they recounted their wanderings in published journals that were full of tales of supernatural wonder and that are, therefore, of interest to those who study the paranormal.

The ancient Greeks pioneered this kind of travel writing, some of which is still in print. Homer's *Odyssey* is the earliest work of this ilk in the Western canon of literature. That epic recounts Odysseus's adventures as, lost, he navigated his way through a mazework of outlandish wonders, some of them blatantly paranormal.

Aristeas was another periparanormalizing wanderer whose poem of travel lore was widely distributed for popular consumption. Pausanius, a second century A.D. medical doctor, wrote a long book recounting his travels to eerie oracles and other spots steeped in supernatural wonder.

Marco Polo (1254–1324), the English Orientalist and explorer Sir Richard Burton (1821–1890), and Robert Ripley, too, are on the honor roll of this club of gallivanting inquirers. In an important respect, the difficulties they met when they presented their observations parallel those faced by all who investigate paranormal phenomena: many of these globe-trotters were scorned by stay-at-home scholars who accused them, often unjustly, of fraud, hoax or—at the very least—of colorful elaboration.

Surely, in the bygone days before the advent of CNN, hyperbole and exaggeration seem to have been a hallmark of their brand of travel literature. The life of the German adventurer and teller of tales Baron von Munchausen (1720–1797) was written in a semifictionalized form in order to parody this type of yarn. His name has become synonymous with a rhetorical style of elaboration and confabulation, tall tale humor that verges on outright fabrication or even on pseudologica fantastica.

Oddly, Munchausen's name has also been taken up into the medical dictionaries to denote another one of those metamaladies, illnesses like hypochondriasis that require of potential sufferers that they already know what illness is. Munchausen's syndrome goes on into a further metasphere of meaning, however, requiring of its impending patients not only that they know what an illness is, but also what a hospital is. Patients with Munchausen's syndrome, who also are known as hospital hoboes, peregrinate from hospital to hospital, seeking admission by presenting with feigned or self-induced pathology. Like hypochondriacs and dysbelieving paranormaliacs, hospital hoboes are undeterred by conditions and situations that would make normal folks desist in their endeavors. As hypochondriacs are immune to medical reassurance, patients afflicted with Munchausen's disorder don't give it up even when they are subjected to the severe pain of surgery or invasive diagnostic procedures.

(Similarly, dysbelievers about the paranormal resist normal canons of language, logic and epistemology, and therefore find it possible to believe what they don't believe. Indeed, not only dysbelievers, but many believers and nonbelievers alike hold to their points of view simply because it is their point of view, not because there is any rational evidence to support it— and indeed, often in spite of evidence to the contrary.)

Though Odysseus, Marco Polo, Sir Richard Burton, and others may not enjoy the best of reputations in terms of their scholarship, meanderers of their breed have made many positive contributions to human knowledge. They were the first to report numerous astonishing phenomena that seemed unbelievable at the time, sometimes putting their discoveries in language that, though perhaps it was the best available under the circumstances, had to be modified and refined in light of later observations.

By its nature, each periparanormal diversion invites its own specific variety of participation, even if only the vicarious one of reading. Periparanormalizers must read or write or converse about such things as ghosts, near-death experiences, dreams that came true, weird happenings in the news, or lands beyond known geographical frontiers; or they must attend a seance, or place a bet, or smoke a joint, or peruse Ripley's cartoons, or submit an item of unusual information to him, or visit an Odditorium, or otherwise engage in some such activity in order to taste any of the periparanormal's odd pleasures of an unknown set at odds with the known.

A. Gambling likes to be there at the most exciting moment of interfacing between the known and the unknown; it is driven to put its money on the line, betting on the precise, suspenseful instant when fate transforms the unknown into the known.

B. Users of psychoactive substances seek ineffably noetic states at the inner frontiers of knowledge.

C. and D. Ripley's work and weird news journalism amuse by presenting their freakish and surprising novelties of knowledge within the epistemic environment of what general knowledge already has learned to expect.

E. Old-timey travel literature enticed by symbolizing the boundary between the known and the unknown as a geographical horizon.

Saying Goodbye to What We Know

To extract the sweet pleasures of the known versus the unknown, the code of the periparanormal allots to each of its subject diversions its own particular set of "bye-laws," that particular pastime's license to say "goodbye" to certain specific provisions of logic or language (or sometimes law!), all for the sake of igniting the exhilarating rush of a seeming clash between knowing and unknowing.

The paranormal, likewise, is permitted to set aside certain provisions of logic or language, cycling between ungrounded figures of speech and empty negations so it can bring us its happy nonsense about life after death, prescience, mind reading, and so on.

- Gambling thinks it can suspend the law of averages, praying that a falling meteorite or a lightning bolt will smite it happy with a mighty impact of money.

- Recreational drug use plays fast and loose with legal restrictions.

- Ripley invoked the privilege that uniquely is a cartoonist's of sketching open a way into other worlds, exotic other places that stagger and please the imagination.

- Weird news practitioners set aside a solemn journalistic stricture when they openly acknowledge that, yes, entertaining is one of journalism's functions, too.

- The ancient genre of travel literature granted its peregrinating authors an exclusive literary license: For a time, each author was reputedly, and on his own word, the only person ever to have been somewhere strange and inaccessibly far away.

The humor that already has been identified as a major tributary of the paranormal runs as a mighty river through the entire periparanormalium.

- Gamblers commonly laugh spontaneously in response to a big win, and casinos book comedians to entertain.

- Alcohol, cannabinols, nitrous oxide, and LSD are among the mind-altering compounds that appeal, in part, because they predispose to mirth.

- Ripley's readers found his cartoons on the comic pages of newspapers.

- Munchausen's name has come to mean tall-tale humor, and printed compilations of weird news are openly humorous in tone.

In fact, it can be said with some justice of the periparanormal that it consists of having fun with unknowns that are funny in almost every one of the senses of the word *funny* that eminent lexicographers list: producing laughter, fun, or amusement; not quite in the best of health or the best of order; queer, curious, peculiar, odd, or strange; unorthodox; comic strip (as in the funnies in the newspapers); and, at an earlier time, tipsy, intoxicated. In short, to periparanormalize is to confront the unknown in a comic spirit.

There Is One More Category, the Largest of All

Having the above structural features in common makes a unified field of the periparanormal. Exactly where in the periparanormal's floor plan does the paranormal itself fit? Or, exactly which compartment in the periparanormal's cabinet of curiosities does the paranormal occupy?

By definition, the paranormal overlaps in part with each of the other constituent activities of the periparanormal. But the paranormal seems to have the most in common with a popular, periparanormal pastime that up to now has remained unnamed: Nonsense Humor. Here is a diversion that, like the paranormal, exults in the sheer fun of nonsense.

The appeal of the paranormal is part humor and part nonsense. So, playful paranormalists infer that the paranormal's appeal closely approximates that of nonsense humor.

Alice in Wonderland, Through the Looking Glass, Flatland, and other works of nonsense humor invite the same, or a similar, kind of seemingly transdimensional wonder that many purportedly paranormal experiences do. Carroll's stories about Alice's voyages into the twilight realm show he was familiar with dysmorphic states precipitated by psychoactive substances and with mirror visions. These two kinds of experiences long have been known to shamans and other practicing paranormalists or periparanormalists.

Benjamin Franklin's chiasmus is right on: "As charms are nonsense, so nonsense is charm." It is a plain fact about nonsense that lots of people like to keep on working on it, trying to whittle as much of the *non* away from it as they can. That is an opening the paranormal and nonsense humor use to amuse with literal and logical absurdities. The constitutive conventions of the periparanormal allow nonsense humor and the paranormal extraordinary liberties with basic, underlying principles of logic and of linguistic meaningfulness.

Proving that nonsense is charming is just a matter of canvassing the ordinary vocabulary of meaninglessness, which contains relatively few words of serious-sounding terminology: absurd, unintelligible, nonsense, meaningless. A few words of ordinary nonsense-speak say mean, nasty things about nonsense by likening it to refuse matter. *Rubbish* and *tommyrot* are words sigh cops and other cynics can use to express their sentiments about the paranormal. And although no prudish playful paranormalist would write them down, ordinary language has a spattering of harsh, crude, coprological synonyms for nonsense that grumble in the same fundaments many funda-Christian dysbelievers about the paranormal do.

But far and away the greatest proportion of ordinary language synonyms for *nonsense* are jocular expressions. It would take a funless fundamentalist, indeed, to miss the affectionate merriment in words like: balderdash, flummery, cockamamie, piffle, humbug, claptrap, bombast, twaddle, twattle, twiddle-twaddle, fiddle-faddle, gabble, gibble-gabble, fiddledeedee, gibberish, hogwash, moonshine, jabberwocky, tomfoolery, fundangle, hooey, hokum, blather, babble, babblement, bibble-babble, gobbledygook, malarkey, rantum-scantum, poppycock, skimble-skamble, falderal, ballyhoo, bunkum, flubdub, fible-fable, baloney, lollygag, flamdoodle, flapdoodle, fiddlesticks, flummadiddle, hocus-pocus, and mumbo jumbo.

I fear that by now some will have concluded that playful paranormalism's position is that the paranormal is just a wispy tuft of silly fluff, with nothing much of substance to it at all. But, no! Gottlob Frege, Bertrand Russell, Ludwig Wittgenstein, C. S. Lewis, Gilbert Ryle, A. J. Ayer, J. L. Austin,

W. V. Quine—a century's worth of great analytic philosophers and logicians—have acknowledged that the concept of nonsense is one of the cardinal ones of philosophy. Together, they have shown that there are numerous useful or otherwise important modes of discourse that nonetheless are nonsensical by various applied standards of verifiability, intelligibility, logic, and ordinary language. Austin condensed many of analytic philosophy's insights into a fine-tuned epiphonema.

> First and most obviously, many "statements" were shown to be, as Kant perhaps first argued systematically, strictly nonsense, despite an unexceptionable grammatical form: and the continual discovery of fresh types of nonsense, unsystematic though their classification and mysterious though their explanation is too often allowed to remain, has done on the whole nothing but good. *(How To Do Things with Words,* Cambridge, MA: Harvard University Press, 1973, page 2.)

Playful paranormalism has demonstrated that the paranormal can be categorized as a popular periparanormal amusement that has a lot in common with nonsense humor. So, the next question is: Is the paranormal an important and useful type of nonsense?

8

JUSTIFYING THE PARANORMAL, OR EVEN THE STUDY OF IT

I want you to know that I recognize what I've done here with my thesis that the paranormal is closely tied to entertainment and diversion. While I believe that this new outlook and this broader contextualization of the paranormal is really the only way we will break the logjam and at last discover anything significant about it, I also understand that, at the same time, I may actually be inhibiting further scholarly study of this subject.

Some scholarly folks who take the paranormal seriously may fret that classifying the paranormal as an amusement maligns the subject. They seem shocked, and may ask, "If the paranormal is just entertainment, how can the serious study of the paranormal be justified?"

But sincere, serious, proparanormal scholars have nothing to fear from playful paranormalism's firm, sincere, and honestly drawn conclusion that the paranormal is nonsense from nowhere. Any misgivings they may have are the illusory by-products of—and by whom—the issue of whether its all worth serious study has been discussed. You see, the problem of justifying scholarly study of the paranormal is not a single issue, but a jumble of issues; a webwork of points in question that are not adequately sorted out and that tend to get confused.

First, there is the issue of entertainment and humor itself.

When the question above is asked (and it frequently is), the playful paranormalist is always startled to hear the word *just* used in the way it always is. The question usually is posed in a tone as if repeating back to him something he had said about the paranormal's being "just entertainment." the word *just* in the question always is spoken as though to put entertainment down. But playful paranormalism never has said anything to the effect that "the paranormal is just entertainment," in that vilifying sense of the word *just* that the questioners are using.

So What's the Matter with Humor?

Playful paranormalism has been admiring and complimenting, *not* badmouthing, the paranormal by pointing out, even emphasizing, its intimacy with humor. Most recipes for happiness list play, humor, and entertainment among the essential ingredients of a good life.

Entertainment often has served the spiritual life well, too, with great works of inspiration. Humor presents complex problems of human nature, and many authorities deny it exists in any earthly species other than our own. Entertainment, play, and humor offer consolation, enjoyment, and release. What's so bad about that?

Besides, playful paranormalism offers an immediate, happy consequence that all sympathetic fans of the paranormal ought to think about. The sigh cops and the demonologists, you know, want to wipe us out—the first group for our sigh crimes and misdemeanors, the second because they suspect us of being their demons. But correctly classifying the paranormal, as playful paranormalism has done, shows why the antiparanormalists' plans for the paranormal's extinction are just not going to get anywhere. The paranormal and humor are kissing cousins, and so the paranormal can no more be excised from the human spirit than can laughter and humor.

As a form of entertainment, the paranormal is pursued for its own sake, as a source of pleasurably exciting and uplifting wonder. Entertainment, provided that it is not harmful, is in need of no further justification than its being what it is. Indeed, it is the paranormal's very kinship with entertainment that is, ultimately, why sigh cops and Christians are driven to fight their battles against it. They do so on quasi-moral grounds, by claiming that the paranormal is positively pestiferous—antiscience or anti-Christ.

Both scientific skeptics and fundamentalists must argue that there are drastic and goshawful consequences in the offing if we, the common people, are permitted to go on in our own merry ways about the paranormal. Our dalliance in these universal human phenomena is, therefore, of urgent concern to them. They foresee dire emergencies they say are now occurring, or are soon to be occurring, in the ordinary world and/or in the supernatural world unless the people's version of the paranormal (whatever it is thought to be) can be squelched or otherwise brought into line with each group's own proposed or imagined standards.

And They're Serious, Too

And these people are not fooling around, either. They are taking themselves very seriously, and expect you to. And folks have been listening. Because, after all, are not our scientists and our preachers among the highest authority figures in the land? And so, many people have been none too careful in the past when thinking about or discussing:

- Whether the paranormal is substantial enough to warrant their serious consideration.

- Whether it is credible, knowable, or just malarkey.

- Whether to allow a course about it to be taught in a university.

- Whether it is or should be legal to study it at all, anywhere.

- Whether someone can be or should be actually punished for studying it, even to the point of being tortured and burnt alive.

The Problem with Thinking about It As a Diversion

The concept of a diversion includes, as a necessary circumstance, that there be one or more ways for people to participate in it as an activity. Correspondingly, the particulars of how someone participates in the paranormal can be a criterion for determining whether the study of the paranormal is justified.

Are we talking about a person with a Ouija board here, or the human subject of a long-term study on clairvoyance? Are we discussing the psychic down the street, or the very real look taken by governments around the world at the use of universal psychic energy? The justification of studying the paranormal varies, from case to case, as a function of how each principal participant, in each case, participates. Playful paranormalists keep their minds and hearts open to the subtleties of participation in the paranormal.

Who the Participants Are
Category 1: The Psychic Fan

The scientific skeptics err when they identify the fandom of the paranormal with the people they think of as keen believers. The group called "fans" is much larger than that.

In addition to the true believers, there are the pseudo-believers, or what I call the "dysbelievers." For this group, the paranormal is a spectator sport.

Dysbelievers, remember, are those who believe what they do not believe. Like the crowd at a wrestling match, they must, in order to enjoy the experience, believe that what they know is not actually happening, is happening.

The dysbelievers each have their own reasons for believing something that they don't believe. If they truly disbelieved, then they would have nothing further to discuss. And true believers and dysbelievers are not the only fans. Fandom also includes those who express their fanship by pseudo-*dis*believing.

These are the rank-and-file, run-of-the-mill, guy-on-the-street skeptics, as opposed to the scientific skeptic. Although they are not authorized to wear the badge of a full-fledged sigh cop, they devote a great deal of time to the paranormal. They love the paranormal because they love to disagree with it.

Pseudo-disbelieving fans spend part of their down time passing information about the paranormal among themselves, reading the *Skeptical Inquirer*, attending skeptical clubs or group discussions, or heckling parapsychologists at lectures, all as a way of amusing themselves by rehashing (again and again) those same old and new tales of supernatural wonder. Although they are fewer in number than pseudo-believing fans, the pseudo-disbelieving ones are just as clearly hobbyists of the subject.

There is also an abundance of grassroots funda-Christians who have a special affinity for the paranormal as an arena in which to play out their favorite combat sport of running down and chasing out demons—any and all demons save their own.

So fandom reflects the three-tiered arrangement of the "expert" controversy.

Category 2: The First-Person Experiencers

But being a fan is not the only way of participating in the paranormal. There is also a category of participants that I will call "first-person experiencers." These are people who have had an encounter with the paranormal that to them is very real, completely authentic, and absolutely undeniable. And this is where I came in, of course. This is how I first became involved in this whole controversy. Because near-death experiences are among the most dramatic of these encounters, and such experiences are fairly prevalent among medical patients who have been resuscitated.

There is also a high incidence of visionary reunions with departed loved ones among the bereaved.

Both types of experiences are very personal and moving, and they can be life-changing.

These experiences provide us with—as I have mentioned before—very little *scientific* knowledge (it is difficult, if not impossible, to verify, and the data is all anecdotal), but a great deal of *practical* knowledge that it is good for a practicing physician or other clinician to have.

Yet none of the three now-entrenched categories of explorers and discussers of this subject—not the parapsychologists, not the skeptics, and not the fundamentalist—are able or willing to respond in an appropriate and humane fashion to persons who express an interest in the paranormal. Thus, while many who become interested in the paranormal do so in the wake of a personal loss, there is no one to whom they can turn at this important and sensitive time.

- Parapsychology has become abstract and intellectualized, and has severed its connection with the human soul. So it often fails to console those who look to it in times of sorrow.

- Scientific skeptics, in their dealings with people who have had unusual, allegedly paranormal experiences, content themselves with pointing out that the experience wasn't what the person having it thought it was at all, but just misfiring neurons, a chemical imbalance, a fantasy, an optical illusion or whatever. So, a person who has had an experience just has to yield to what must be presumed to be the superior insight and wisdom of a sigh cop, who usually hasn't had the experience.

- Fervent fundamentalists see nothing amiss in preaching to Aunt Florene, bereft and kindly and fragile though she may be, that it was not really the spirit of Uncle Hamperd who visited her last week to comfort her and to tell her where he put those important papers. No, it was actually a malignant demon disguised as Uncle Hamperd, there to lure her into hell, so she had better go home and read the Bible. Not the one that she keeps at her bedside, though, because that one was translated by scholars who were laboring under Satanic influence. Let her use this here King James Version instead, because it's written down exactly as God dictated it in England, during the height of the witchcraft persecutions.

It's a good thing the fundamentalists always say these things only in a spirit of "Christian" love. Otherwise, it might appear that their words were cruel or insulting, or even as though their religion were based not in the warm places of the heart, as the whole of the Bible Brigade declares it to be, but in the cold, distant, and airy reaches of the intellect, along with Communism!

Is Study of the Paranormal Justified?

When being asked whether the study of the paranormal can be justified or not, dysbelievers never pause first to think through the important and unresolved preliminary issue of exactly *whose* paranormal is in question. Precisely which category of participants are we discussing here? Which are we proposing to use as a context within which to consider the question of serious study? Rather than address this question, each official dysbeliever arrives at the conference with their own preferred word with its stipulated meaning. Yet all the parties are arguing as if they were talking about one and the same thing.

Back to Words Again

I said earlier that the problem of justifying scholarly study of the paranormal is not a single issue, but a jumble of issues; a webwork of points in question that are not adequately sorted out and that tend to get confused. Then, first, we looked at the issue of entertainment and humor. There is also the issue of vocabulary.

It already has been shown how, in order to graft belief or disbelief onto the paranormal, that the vocabulary with which the subject of the alluringly unknown is discussed first has to be remodeled, always to the specifications of one or another of the dysbelievers.

Yet, however any of the disbelieving paranormalists trim the paranormal of what he or she affirms to be its excess meanings, all that linguistic fat just keeps growing back. And since most of the fat that always reappears is the real fun of the paranormal, ordinary language takes the position that the paranormal has strong family ties to humor, diversion, and play. In other words, as we have amply shown here, the words regular people use to talk about the paranormal give ample evidence of what they think about it, and what they hold to be true—even if they don't do so consciously: we intuitively know and understand and accept the connection between the paranormal and entertainment.

Until the experts have something better to offer, therefore, ordinary language remains the best set of directions for thinking and talking about the paranormal. So, playful paranormalism maintains that it is this, the entire ordinary vocabulary of the oddly unknown, that first must pass professorial muster in order for the paranormal to gain entrance into academe.

It is the position of playful paranormalism that what is ordinarily talked about as the paranormal—in the way that it is ordinarily talked about—should be the subject of serious study. This extraordinary declaration in support of the ordinary paranormal's candidacy for scholarship may raise additional red flags in the minds of scholars who favor taking the paranormal as a serious subject.

Some may feel that, like categorizing it as entertainment, this additional consideration also puts the subject down. Perhaps they feel that equating the paranormal with the other subjects that we use ordinary language to talk about would make the paranormal something unworthy of scholarship—that a "scholarly paranormal" must be as the experts define it. But there it is again, that same old trouble. Who on earth are the "experts" on the paranormal?

Justifying the Paranormal Itself

This is not a small question, because, for many, the issue of justifying serious study of the paranormal is merged, mentally, with the issue of justifying the paranormal itself.

The problem seems to be whether the paranormal can be justified as a field of knowledge, or as a source of knowledge. These are two entirely different issues, incidently, with the answer depending on who we are recognizing the "experts" to be.

Each of the two sets of antiparanormal dysbelievers—the scientific skeptics and the fundamentalists—want us to know that it (and it alone) has at its exclusive disposal the very knowledge necessary for stemming, holding back, or reversing the ever-rising tides of superstition or the occult. Then, the parapsychologically dysbelieving muddle into the morass with their counterclaim that, no, it is they, and not the skeptics, who represent the best of the paranormal that the scientific spirit has to offer. They chime in with their same old song that soon the paranormal will be tied down scientifically into new knowledge.

Muddying the Discussion

The ongoing discussion of whether study of the paranormal can be justified, as that discussion is conducted customarily, invariably confounds that issue with the question of whether the occurrence of paranormal phenomena can be confirmed scientifically.

Scientific skeptics conceive of the paranormal as something atavistic and sterile as compared to science. Playful paranormalism concurs in this assessment in-so-far as the study of the paranormal is confined by the limitations of the discussion that we have been pointing to throughout this book. As I have said over and over again, no advances have ever come out of that discussion, which has taken place within the frameworks having been set by the big three, and using the vocabulary upon which they have agreed (as opposed to that which is commonly used by regular people).

To repeat the argument of this entire book, the orthodox controversy is too set in its ways. It has become its own fixed model (and an unproductive one at that) for how ideas about the paranormal are to be bounced off one another.

The experts never give the ordinary language paranormal a turn at bat, never ask it to tell its own story of what it has learned, or how. And those experts also never allow playful paranormalists at the table.

Yet, according to playful paranormalist teachings, the ordinary paranormal actually has come up with an immensity of new knowledge over the ages by going about things in its own way.

Initially, it may seem inconsistent for a playful paranormalist to justify the paranormal by making out a case that sometimes the paranormal does bear new knowledge. For just as saying that one believes something, is, in part, saying that it is true, so also saying that one knows something, is, in part, saying that it is true.

And playful paranormalism has already satisfied itself that there is no truth to be had in the paranormal, nor any falsity, either. Instead, there is an assortment of excellent, weird, anomalous, wondrous, strange, bizarre, uncanny, eerie, marvelous, literally nonsensical unknowns, sugared and peppered with wacky and goofy humor.

Although the language of the alluringly unknown neither speaks truth, nor serves as a repository of truth, it does incubate truth.

This language is a seething, simmering stew pot of meanings attempting to come to terms with a lot of wondrous, weird, eerie, marvelous feelings about an unknown that is trying to get a foothold within knowns that lean in the opposite direction. This, in spite of the fact that those oppositely leaning knowns are as well and as certainly known as anything is about the privacy of thought, about the future, or about death. So, even though what is either true or false does not reside in the literal nonsense that is the paranormal, newly determinable meanings do manage to bubble forth from that linguistic broth as, over the centuries, the ordinary vocabulary of the paranormal is used to talk over near-death experiences, ghosts, premonitions, telepathy, and reincarnation again and again and again.

And more than new meanings. Also, in truth, new knowledge.

The Ultimate Justification

Here is the ultimate justification for both the paranormal, and the serious study of it: it is, in fact, a source, and not merely a field, of knowledge. It produces "new knowing"— though it is not always credited for it, as we shall soon see.

Here is how it has worked: over long stretches of time, a few of the paranormal's drifty fragments of nonsense, illuminated by someone's flashes of insight, have been able to be pinned down to meanings that are specifiable enough to be found either true or false. In that way the paranormal has, from time to time, been induced to deliver on its long-standing promise of some new knowings.

An example of the new knowledge that gradually has oozed out of the paranormal over long periods may be found in the Muses. These paranormally creative spirits of long centuries of Greek antiquity were consulted at their museions (places people went when they were wishing for creative inspiration).

It was Aristotle who dreamed up a super-museion, a fabulous attraction where the learned could be kept to themselves, fed and housed free of charge, exempted from taxes and provided with a huge library, all so that they could spend their time staying on the good side of the Muses. That plan was carried out after Aristotle's pupil, Alexander, conquered Egypt, where the great Museion of Alexandria was founded.

It would take a big book to relate the story of how many bushels of knowledge of how many kinds are attributed to the many musers that mused in the Museion, but even one example can serve to indicate something of that institution's immeasurable importance. There, the mechanical genius Ctepios (285–247 B.C.) invented the metal spring, the pump, the pipe organ, the musical keyboard, and the mechanical clock.

When the paranormal is placed within the broader context of the periparanormal as a whole, all those clever ways of having fun with concepts of knowledge have added up to lots of major discoveries. Remember how we listed gambling as one of the classifications of the periparanormal? Well, gambling has some of its roots in common with the paranormal, and since probability theory first was thought out by a determined compulsive gambler, it is partly an offshoot of the paranormal.

Big wishing is one of the paranormal's occupational diseases, another condition it shares with gambling. The paranormal also has been mixed up with gambling in the lives and careers of the biggest wishers of all, the alchemists of medieval times.

They worked phenomena that still are thought of as paranormal—mirror gazing and divination, for example—into some dim beginnings of experimental technique. Using furnaces, retorts and glass vessels, and whatever substances that were to be had, they aimed it all toward the two prospects that always seemed to the alchemists to be so imminent of realization: discovering a formula for prolonging life to an unending length, and creating infinite financial plentitude by turning stuff into gold. Yet the actual effects that the alchemists' pursuits had on their own and their families' financial situations were the same as those of compulsive gamblers. As Charles Mackay wrote about alchemist Bernard of Treves (1406–1490):

> In the search of his chimera nothing could daunt him. Repeated disappointment never diminished his hopes; and from the age of fourteen to that of eighty-five he was incessantly employed among the drugs and furnaces of his laboratory, wasting his life with the view of prolonging it, and reducing himself to beggary in the hopes of growing rich. *(Extraordinary Popular Delusions and the Madness of Crowds,* New York: Barnes & Noble Books, 1993, page 131.)

And yet, as alchemy blended the paranormal, wishing, and gambling over centuries, little bits of new alchemical meaning were churned up here and there that eventually were translated into good chemistry.

Is Much of Modern Math a Product of the Paranormal?

On occasion, the paranormal erupts in a mind-geyser of new knowing, spewing forth entirely new sciences overnight.

Consider the case of Rene Descartes, and what happened to him (or through him) on November 10, 1619. He was twenty-three years old at that time, and had shut himself in for a day and a night in a room heated by a stove. He had resolved to spend that interlude trying to come to an understanding of how to get at the truth.

It was no record hibernation, not one for the Guinness Books, but he cooked a big batch of new knowledge for so short a stay in that room. Confined there in his chamber, he came down with a mind fever of new knowingness. His thoughts raced around in a mind whirlwind that Descartes (writing of himself as he did in the third person) said "threw his mind into violent agitations that grew greater and greater" until he fell into a state of "enthusiasm."

During the daylight hours, he had an astonishing, mathematical vision-revelation of epistemological insight, the exact nature and content of which is not clear, probably because visionary experiences typically are ineffable, not translatable into ordinary talk. The gist of his vision persists, though, for what he envisioned that day was the development of the relations between geometry and algebra, and that was how he came to lay the foundation of analytic geometry, and to formulate the principle of mathematization of all the quantifiable sciences.

As if that was not evidence enough of the role of the paranormal in this revelation, that night his daytime vision of mathematical epistemology reverberated in three successive, powerful aftershocks—three dreams from within which Descartes, still asleep, asked himself whether he was dreaming or having visions.

Descartes wrote that he could only imagine the dream had come to him "from above." Descartes had no doubt that "it was the Spirit of Truth which had wanted to open" to him the "treasures of all the sciences by this dream." He took the dreams as a command from on high that he seek truth by applying the mathematical method.

During the intervening centuries, a towering mountain of new knowledge has arisen, the upthrust of Descartes' famous mindquake. It is widely appreciated that by living through the process of *ergo's* making *sum*-thing out of his *cogito*, Descartes was the first to define mind in the modern manner—as awareness. Unfairly, however, the paranormal usually gets no respect at all for its decisive contribution to Descartes' great awakening of the scientific spirit.

More Justification: Others through Whom the Paranormal Has Produced New Knowing

Other times, something has shaped itself into new knowledge by bouncing off the paranormal or another periparanormal diversion, as off a backboard.

When Strabo (63 B.C.-25 A.D.) founded scientific geography, he set the popular writings of literary peregrinators to one side. He dropped their wonder-filled narratives about travel to faraway, unknown regions into a box labeled "entertainment."

Strabo put the works of poetical mundivagants like Aristeas in there, along with Homer's story of Odysseus's voyages, and many others. In short, modern geography sprang into existence by using fanciful travel literature as a backstop. It was an event of that sort that gave birth to academe, the institution of higher learning that has persisted in an unbroken tradition ever since.

Socrates (469-399 B.C.) made a reputation for himself as a man with a rigorous and inquiring mind who thirsted for knowledge, but by his diligent search for it, he had only persuaded himself of his own ignorance. Like-minded students of philosophy attached themselves to him and followed in his footsteps as he walked the streets of Athens in pursuit of wisdom.

One of these hangers-on, a young man named Chaerephon, decided to travel to the Oracle of Delphi, a renowned fortune-telling establishment high on a mountainside north of Athens, to find out what light Apollo, the deity who spoke through that place, could shed on Socrates's spectacular talent for deep thinking.

By the standards of contemporary industrialized societies, the Delphic procedure for consulting Apollo was just about as paranormal as anyone can imagine. A woman, specially selected for the great honor from among a small number of proud, local families, was secreted away in a private compartment within a temple, where petitioners' questions were put to her for the god's consideration. She was suspended from a metal tripod over a crevice from which arose an aromatic maze of psychoactive vapors. When the prophetess had breathed herself into a precognitive swoon, or delirium, the attendants reeled her back in. Then they tried to make sense of the god's advice by casting the seeress's inspired babblings into common Greek language. The answer that Apollo gave Chaerephon through the prophetess was, "No man is wiser than Socrates."

When this information got back to Athens, no one was more surprised and baffled by it than Socrates himself, who thought of himself as an ever-ignorant person who understood hardly anything. But there was a sacred tradition that the gods always spoke the truth through their oracles, so no one would doubt that the statement "No man is wiser than Socrates" was true.

The slippery part about the oracles' sayings was not determining whether they were true, but determining exactly what the oracle *meant* by its words. So, Socrates set out on his mission to find out exactly what was the oracle's sense or meaning of the statement, "No man is wiser than Socrates."

Socrates canvassed Athens, asking questions of every person who was popularly reputed (or self-reputed) to be wise. Socrates was the inventor of careful cross-examination, and he soon discovered that, after a few of his penetrating questions, every single noteworthy knower or sage of Athens quickly became nonplussed. So, Socrates concluded that those who claimed to be wise or who thought that they had knowledge actually were mistaken. Socrates, however, was fully aware that he had no knowledge, so he realized that what the oracle must have meant was that wisdom consists of knowing that one does not know.

It is commonplace for skeptical commentators on divination to explain that a client's ingenuity in reading a fitting meaning into a fortune-teller's words can be as vital a factor in a prophecy's seeming to come true as any paranormal talent the fortune-teller has. Unquestionably, it was Socrates's own brilliant inventiveness that gave us the Socratic method that has been bringing so much new knowledge out into the open for so long a time. The point, though, is that something that plainly was paranormal in its nature and inception was present as a stable platform upon which Socrates's insights were able to sculpt themselves into a powerful new technique for getting at the truth.

Socrates's student, Plato, institutionalized his master's plan for dogged crossinterrogation into academe, an organization of scholars determined to pass on a tradition of learning well grounded in constant and resolute self-doubting. So, even if the paranormal's role in that epoch-making event was only that of a foil, it nonetheless was a foil that had to be there at the origin of something that has been very good for humanity.

Has the Paranormal Birthed Not Only Modern Math, but Philosophy, Too?

About a century and a half earlier, the paranormal had attended the birth of philosophy itself. Thales of Miletus (625-545 B.C.), the man who is regarded as the first philosopher and the founder of science, is credited with predicting an eclipse of the sun that took place in May, 585 B.C. Some historians are of the opinion that at that time Thales could not really have had either sufficient information or an adequate methodology for forecasting an eclipse, so perhaps his success was just happy happenstance. But that is beside the point that people of the time celebrated Thales's accomplishment as being one of a man of learning, a scholar and a thinker, and that meant that those people did not attribute what Thales did to a paranormal power of divination.

The discipline of philosophy that Thales instigated is known as the mother of the sciences. Almost every other academically established field or branch of learning developed out of philosophy as philosophers learned to hone their questions more sharply, and to devise new ways of answering them. But the paranormal was there at the birth of philosophy as an antipode, the preextant podium from which the arrival of a new nondivinatory, bookish mode of determining what is true or false could be announced to the world.

So, in terms of its own history, the ordinary paranormal has done pretty well for itself as a provider of new knowledge. Over the ages, it has made a pretty good showing of new knowledge; it has proven itself to be a sometime-begetter of new truth. In the long run, it has proven advantageous to keep the ordinary language of the alluringly unknown open as an option for thinking. And the fact that a form of popular entertainment enacted through the use of a confederacy of ordinary meanings sometimes could find out something new and interesting is enough to make a playful paranormalist sit up and take notice.

The argument of this chapter has shown that, in terms of truth, the vocabulary of the alluringly unknown is not only a poetic language, it is a poietic language, too, if it be given plenty of time. What it is not is a literal language.

Playful paranormalists respectfully acknowledge that honest and sincere relations or narrations of the paranormal, by their nature, are thought, written, and spoken in a figurative language of multicomplicated meaning, not in the literal language belief or disbelief require. So, naturally, playful paranormalists want to know more about the kind of figuration involved in the paranormal.

The paranormal's special bent for spatial figuration, its failure to make literal sense, its reflexive self-negation, its aptitude in the long term for turning up novelties of truth from a well-plowed field of old knowledge: they all come together in the concept of *pretergression,* as a beneficial transaction of language that can be made by the use of the ordinary vocabulary of the alluringly unknown. *Pretergression* is defined as the action of going beyond bounds or limits, or as the failure to conform to a principle, rule, law, or regulation.

Pretergression is a notion that can unify the paranormal, conceptually. A great proportion of those who have thought a lot about humor think its essence is incongruity, a transgression of limits; so pretergression can account for the paranormal's funny nonsense. The paranormal is a game of rule-breaking; so pretergression can account for the paranormal's rebellious streak. It can account also for the paranormal's syncretic action of truth-formation. It is through pretergression that the paranormal establishes a lasting relationship between entertainment value and truth value. Pretergression amuses and bemuses as, with glacial force, it thrusts new truths up above a landscape of old knowledge.

Because it brings new truth into being, pretergression could even be thought of as a figure of action. Over the centuries, that is, the vocabulary of the alluringly unknown pretergresses new truth out of old knowledge. And that justifies the paranormal as a source of new knowledge.

The argument is over at last.

9

THE RHETORIC OF DYSBELIEF

Justifying the paranormal as a source of new knowledge is not sufficient to justify it as a new field of knowledge, however. Given all its credentials, it seems odd that the ordinary paranormal has gone so long and so far without being granted academic status.

To a playful paranormalist, it seems a shame that all those eager students who want some higher education about the ordinary paranormal aren't allowed it, in large part because of the disgrace of "scholarship" that is the dysbelievers' controversy. It's time someone raises some questions about that old, tiffy commotion.

If the paranormal is properly classified as a species of popular entertainment, why don't the works of recognized experts in the field read more like the works of the qualified scholarly experts on entertainment, the theater, or literature? How is the existence of that studied tradition that has long passed itself off as learned disputation about the paranormal to be explained?

Simple. It has been a closed discussion, as we have been noting from the very beginning. A closed discussion by a closed circle of three, using a closed, limited, and literal vocabulary. Thus, the discussion has itself created a roadblock, precluding any further or deeper understanding of the very subject it proposes to explore, and leaving the inquiring public hanging on the tines of a false trilemma.

One problem is that there has been no "metalevel" formulation of the traditional controversy. *Metalevel* is the best word I have to express this notion. There is no body of sustained or systematic argumentation or deliberation about the accepted guidelines themselves. This book is an effort to establish just that.

Until now, no one has seriously challenged the parapsychologists, the scientific skeptics, and the fundamentalists, nor the points of view they have espoused, much less the method and the manner by which they have arrived at them. No commentators have come around asking to see triply dysbelieving paranormalism's original blueprints of disputation, or to check out its patent on the process, or to inspect its foundations, to determine if they are firmly grounded in rationality.

We've said all this before, and so may now seem to be belaboring the point, but it is of resounding importance for all serious, nondysbelieving students of the paranormal to be on their toes at this point. They must remain acutely aware that the paranormal's conventions of ordinary meaning are silent about whether or how to study the paranormal properly.

We emphasize again, therefore, that there is a set of ordinances that usually are brought automatically into play when anyone brings the paranormal up for serious conversation or disputation. This is the built-in conventional wisdom of the situation (actually an ancient rhetorical tradition) that establishes a panel of three chairs to be filled, and appoints the three functionaries who are to fill them. That is, there is an implicit convention in place, a stipulation to the effect that each of the three widely recognized parties is entitled to its say, and it is the unspoken general understanding that in a paranormal turn of the conversation, it usually is that triune of dysbelievers that most folks will look to for some expert words or opinions.

That presumption generally is familiar to the segment of the lay public that is highly interested in the paranormal and also is adhered to by the trio of dysbeliever-experts as their general guidelines for disputation. So almost every time the paranormal is brought up for serious consideration, the discourse slips right into gear with the dysbelievers' continuing arguments. Unfortunately, when serious talk turns to the paranormal, the bureaucracy of the three dysbelievings usually gets wind of the situation immediately and dispatches its agents to the scene in a hurry, where they insist that all three sets of their complicated forms be filled out promptly and correctly, according to all their conflicting instructions.

Maintaining the Stalemate

What is this all about? Why is this happening?

It is happening because each of the big three discussers of the paranormal have a deep investment in keeping the discussion going—but going nowhere. It is about maintaining the stalemate.

All of those separate, superadded conventions, stipulations, presumptions, opinions of conventional wisdom, automatic responses, and general understandings—all of them—are there to steer the controversy about the paranormal along the same course it has been taking for far too long. All those additional provisions guarantee that the controversy will keep on running along smoothly, forever *in median res,* always in the middle of the action. All precepts of that nature help bind the listener's or reader's fancy to that gripping, griping old controversy by lending a dramatic flair to its recurrent confrontations.

It is important to understand that these are entirely different orders and kinds of conventions than are those rules and regulations of the ordinary language of the paranormal, the ordinary uses of the vocabulary of the alluringly unknown that makes up the paranormal's wordfest of meanings.

In other words, the big three discussers keep the discussion going nowhere simply by the way they are talking about it. And since no one else has been allowed, by convention, into the discussion to add to the dialogue, the discussion itself goes in circles.

The set of conventions, regulations, stipulations, and so on, that favors the dysbelievers' controversy does not logically follow from the first, prior set of conventions, regulations, stipulations, and so forth, those that govern the ordinary use of the vocabulary of the alluringly unknown—at least not as far as playful paranormalism has been able to discover. Put simply, the way the big three are talking about the paranormal has nothing to do with the way ordinary people, using ordinary language, talk about it. The conventional wisdom discussions—the conversations of the people so many turn to for insight about all of this—turn out to bear little or no relationship to the conversations of ordinary language paranormalism. The "experts" in parapsychology, science, and religion are coming from a place that does not logically follow from the place in which ordinary people find themselves vis-à-vis the paranormal.

What we have here is two distinct populations talking about the same subject, but in a distinctly different way.

Dysbelievers in the big three cannot drop their posturing and talk about the paranormal in a normal way, because to do so would be to lose nearly all of their arguments before they state them. Superficially, at least, the circumstances would seem rather to weigh against any dysbeliever or any set of dysbelievers using logically the ordinary language of the paranormal precisely because each dysbeliever gets started by separating just one word and one meaning out of the ordinary vocabulary of the alluringly unknown's extensive collection of paranormalabilia, and then blowing that word and meaning up out of all proportion. Thus, they communicate with rhetoric, rather than logic. It is the only way they can win the argument.

Dysbelievers begin—and, perforce, must begin—by setting themselves against the ordinary language of the paranormal, seizing on one word with a preferred meaning. Then, by coupling its one-word meaning with pseudo-believing or with pseudo-disbelieving, each dysbelieving sets itself up for a sure and certain fall.

But here is something interesting. In spite of the fact that dysbelievers use language in an entirely different way, it does seem that the dysbelievers' controversy, with all its extra, cumbersome regulations, manages somehow to coexist in some degree of uneasy harmony or parallelism with the ordinary language's paranormal.

How does this come about? What are the relationships between the dysbelievers' version of the paranormal, as referred to in their continuing discussions, and the everyday, ordinary language paranormal?

Are we talking in two different ways about the same thing, or are we talking about two different things?

Let's take a look.

Inasmuch as it is rhetorical rather than logical, the standing controversy can fairly be subjected to a rhetorical critique. I want to make it crystal clear, however, that I am referring to rhetoric in an honorific way, not in any of the several uncomplimentary or debasing senses of the word.

Rhetoric is the ancient and respectable art of figurative, specialized, prosaic, or poetic uses of language. It is the discipline that formulates the rules of language, by which eloquent or effective expression is achieved.

Playful paranormalists prefer logic to rhetoric, so I am asking readers to allow me the luxury of abbreviating the following treatment. I will sketch out a brief description of the rhetoric of just one sect of dysbelievers to spare myself extra wearisome labor. However, the principle of exposition I use with the one could be applied mutatis mutandis to the other two. Perhaps some other scholarly paranormalist some day will contribute the needed additions.

The Way the Big Three Talk about the Paranormal

The rhetoric of a dysbeliever could accurately be schematized in numerous distinct, nonmutually exclusive ways. I will confine my illustrative sketch to three aspects: vocabulary, speech acts, and speaker style.

- The vocabulary of a dysbeliever is the list of words that its proponents specifically bring into the controversy as their own characteristic contribution.

- A dysbeliever's speech acts are the actions that he or she specifically performs by the use of the words of their particular vocabulary as they carry on their characteristic kind of discourse about the paranormal.

- Speaker style is the characteristic manner in which a speaking or writing dysbeliever of a particular persuasion (parapsychologist, skeptic, or fundamentalist) carries on discourse about the paranormal, and this includes not only the dysbeliever's mannerisms of presentation, but also how the speaker or writer usually comes across to others, or the typical or intended effects on others.

Parapsychologists and skeptics cast most of their stones at each other, so I am going to make an example of the funda-Christians, who have been getting off scot free while casting their stones at anyone with different positions than their own.

Vocabulary

The cant of funda-Christian dysbelievers consists of those words that fundamentalist authorities on the paranormal most frequently and characteristically resort to when they fulminate on the subject: Satan, devil, demons, (eternal) damnation, condemnation, deception.

Speech Acts

In terms of their illocutionary force (the speech acts that typically are performed by their use), several of those words are imprecations and maledictions. *hell, damn* and *devil* frequently are used as curse words. Imprecation and malediction are uses of language that invoke or call down evil on others. Damning or condemning is to pronounce someone guilty. Maledictions or imprecations are used for denouncing or censuring someone publicly. Such words are expressions of anger, contempt, hatred, or hostility. So, basically, when funda-Christians tell us sincere, innocent proparanormalist investigators or fans that we are agents of Satan, or that we are going to hell, they are cursing us and are venting their rage and hostility on us.

Speaker Style

The rhetorical style of funda-Christian speakers and writers on the paranormal is minatory and it is top-heavy with cocky self-assurance. Fundamentalist speakers on the subject come across as puffed up; they feel certain they have all the answers. They often appear disdainful and scornful of those who have different opinions. Their presentations are expostulatory. To a compliant, weak-willed, or passive-dependent hearer or reader, funda-Christian expostulators probably seem intimidating. The typical fiery, funda-Christian, antiparanormal dysbeliever holds a prop in his hand—a Bible—and he waves it about as someone would who was about to use it as a bludgeon.

Now I said earlier that the points I am making about the language, acts, and style of the fundamentalists can be made about the other two of the big three discussers as well, and they can. For the largest point I am making here about the approach to the subject of the paranormal of all three is that their argument continues to hold center court precisely because of its rhetorical, dramatic, literary, and amusive qualities.

Cursing others to hell is a powerful, dramatic, attention-getting speech-act. Parapsychologists and scientific skeptics, likewise, have their powerful, dramatic ways of getting people to pay attention to what they are saying.

The paranormal of dysbelievers exists side-by-side with what I call ordinary paranormal (what is really experienced and is really talked about in real language by real people) because the dysbelievers capture our attention with their rhetoric. We are entertained by it—by all their frothing and denying and denunciations. Yes, even being cursed, or hearing others being cursed, can be titillating, and even slightly amusing. For many people, hearing others cursing is entertaining, and cursing is a great way to let off steam (which is exactly what fired-up, uptight funda-Christians need to do).

Dysbelieving paranormalism exists alongside ordinary paranormalism because it is in tune with people's desire for fun with the paranormal, not in virtue of its being an effective organon for securing new knowledge about the paranormal. Left to itself over the centuries, the ordinary paranormal has had a pretty good record of bringing forth new knowledge. Such is not the case with the discussions and explorations that have been undertaken by the dysbelievers, however. Not only can the big three discussers not come up with anything new, they can't even agree among themselves about the old.

Over the long centuries of their domination of this controversy, their antique rhetorical plan has definitively proven itself to be an inadequate means of attaining consensus about the paranormal. Nonetheless, for the reasons I've just given, it is well entrenched and all-pervasive; its tentacles spread out into the media, and almost all of the fans of the paranormal pay homage to it, also.

In general, the press falls for the mandates of the controversy hook, line, and sinker. Journalists arrive to interview experts on the paranormal wondering, "Believer or disbeliever?" or, worse yet, assuming they already know. If they think that the "expert" they have come to interview is a believer, they will come forearmed with the standard "skeptical" questions, questions that already are steeped in the inequities of dysbelieving.

The talk shows have fallen in love with dysbelieving about the paranormal, too. Because it is mock-rational and theatrical, the dysbelievers' controversy makes for just the kind of dramatic confrontation that can catch and hold viewers' or listeners' attention.

Is There Any Hope?

Perhaps I'm a pessimist at heart. The insights and arguments that I've brought forth in this book notwithstanding, I see that the dysbelievers' controversy is deep-dyed, and playful paranormalism feels destined to have no impact on it whatsoever. I do not base my assessment on mere pessimism alone, however. For I have looked into my crystal ball, and I have foreseen only more of the same for that old melee. I have foreseen that parapsychologists will hail playful paranormalism's findings insofar as those findings pertain to the keystone skeptics, but that those same parapsychologists will experience playful paranormalism's findings not so much to their liking insofar as those findings pertain to parapsychology.

I have also foreseen that many sigh cops may applaud playful paranormalism's insights about parapsychology, but that those same "skepticops" will refrain from applauding playful paranormalism's own, more skeptical heresies, especially the ones about the sigh cops themselves. I have further foreseen that some countable number of parapsychologists and some countable number of scientific skeptics will count themselves in general agreement with playful paranormalism's account of fundamentalist preachings about the paranormal.

Finally, I have foreseen that not even one fundamentalist will approve of what playful paranormalism has had to say about demonology, though probably many Christians will.

Fandom, journalism, and the media may cotton to the way the dysbelievers disagree and dispute about the paranormal, but playful paranormalists stay entirely clear of that kind of misthinking. Playful paranormalism has found out enough about dysbelieving that it wants to make doubly sure it never gets sucked into the mind-whirlpool of an unending runaround of three silly self-rightnesses.

Playful paranormalism has been methodically burning each best-known bridge of the paranormal behind it until it has argued itself now into a staunch fortress of nonbelief. Therefore, playful paranormalism hereby declares its own independence from the controversy about the paranormal as it always has been argued.

Still, We Must Try to Have the Last Laugh

My pessimism aside, wouldn't it be great to have the last laugh on all of this? Wouldn't it be fabulous to take the parapsychologists, the scientific skeptics, and the fundamentalists to task for not allowing others into the centuries-long discussion on the paranormal? Wouldn't it be great to throw open a new door, break through an old barrier, bring in another perspective on this subject?

And wouldn't it be productive to undertake a serious, scholarly exploration of the ordinary paranormal, as opposed to the paranormal that the big three have devised out of their linguistic and contextual distortions?

Playful paranormalism does consider the paranormal to be an important subject that is susceptible to rational study and even, within limits, to systematic study.

What would it take to forge paranormalistics into a viable discipline, and, eventually, possibly an academically respectable discipline?

Playful paranormalism holds that it would require:

- Acknowledging the relationship between the paranormal and humor, play and entertainment.

- Respectfully owning up to that relationship.

- Reasoning carefully as to its implications.

The conceptual, historical, and linguistic territory of entertainment, play and humor could become a natural bridge over which serious, nondysbelieving discourse would be able to pass into a rational process of academic scholarship.

BUT . . .

10

THE ONLY WAY A SERIOUS STUDY OF THE PARANORMAL WILL BE LEGITIMIZED

If the paranormal is ever to become a subject fit for higher learning, the serious, scholarly discourse on the subject must somehow achieve escape velocity from the well-known, time-worn controversy created by the long-standing conventions we have described here. Alternative perspectives must be considered, and unasked questions must at last be addressed through a new, expanded psychology of the paranormal.

It is up to playful paranormalism to take some of these neglected points of view under consideration and to undertake these inquiries, with an eye toward determining what, if anything, new and useful they can offer.

Who holds some of these points of view?

The Hero Club Members

A hero club of the paranormal is an organization that singles out for its special attention the purportedly paranormal experiences or abilities of a revered hero figure of the past, or that focuses on its hero's theories or ideas about the paranormal. Members take great pleasure in rehearsing the life story of the hero again and again, feasting on anecdotes about the paranormal wonders the hero is given credit for accomplishing or elucidating. A few in each membership tend to be suspicious about paranormal talents or phenomena other than those officially attributed to the hero or endorsed by that idolized person. Paranormal hero movements maintain documents about their heroes, preserve collections of their heroes' writings, and act to keep the memories of their revered central figures alive. As time passes, these alliances may assume something of the flavor of religions.

Such movements have grown up around Sai Baba and Paramahansa Yogananda. Both men are said to have performed paranormal feats and to have received extraordinary insights from an other-than-normal source. These feats and insights caused others to form spiritual movements around these men.

Similar in nature, although perhaps somewhat more secular, are the organizations created around Edgar Cayce and C. G. Jung, and even more contemporarily, the over two hundred study groups formed around the world to explore the writings of the aforementioned Neale Donald Walsch, who declares himself to have had in 1992 the decidedly paranormal experience of a two-way conversation with God. Members of all of these groups usually are seeming believers.

Seemingly disbelieving in the paranormal is represented in the skeptical movement that sprang up around Houdini. The movement that, long ago, organized to perpetuate and to celebrate the paranormality of Emmanuel Swedenborg is now formally a religion.

Dysbelieving is a fact of life among the members of the paranormal hero clubs, so in that sense they have nothing novel to contribute to the study of the paranormal. I can attest from long personal experience that the people in the groups I have named all are extraordinarily nice folk. They are to be strongly commended for their great generosity in providing archival services and for providing a forum for public discussion.

Courageous Psychotherapists

Playful paranormalism can present a united front with the courageous psychotherapists who have bucked orthodoxy by accepting that having paranormal and spiritual experiences is an important and meaningful concomitant of being human. Although these therapists avoid the mistake of lumping the paranormal with the abnormal, they acknowledge that persons who have paranormal or spiritual experiences may benefit from counseling—both to help them integrate their experiences and to support them as they learn to cope with the ridicule that sometimes is heaped upon them by the uninformed.

Playful paranormalism can go along with this approach, with the proviso that it be understood that psychotherapy itself is a peripherally periparanormal enterprise. There is a lack of sound scientific evidence for the efficacy of psychotherapy, just as there is a lack of sound scientific evidence for the paranormal. Certain puzzling, nonordinary states of awareness—dissociation, hypnosis, even certain kinds of delirious episodes—pertain as much to the study of the paranormal as they do to the expertise of the psychotherapist. The paranormal and psychotherapy share a common history that converges in such ancient concepts as divination, which was thought of as a form of mental disturbance, as well as a way of foretelling the future and of assessing another person's character. Like the paranormal, psychotherapy can become a pastime, especially after a few years of it.

The internationally famous psychiatrist, Stanislav Grof has been influential in organizing psychotherapists who are receptive to their clients' paranormal or spiritual experiences into the Transpersonal Psychology Association. Its members are mindful that the psychological issues about paranormal experience aren't ontological, but are clinical and phenomenological.

Wishful Thinkers

The sigh cops are forever trying to arrest us scholarly proparanormalists, whether we are pseudo-believing ones or not, on that catch-all charge of wishful thinking. And the playful paranormalist would brook no denial that wishing has always been one of the paranormal's major preoccupations. The alchemists' quest for a source of infinite plenty is still alive in the various plans New Agers promote for "visualizing" one's way into the big bucks.

The scientific skeptics aren't immune to the wishing fevers that infect paranormalizers, either. The sigh cops recently mailed out an urgent solicitation begging their membership for money. They think the high rate of sigh crime threatens at any minute to overwhelm the scientific world order, and they say they need cash to put a stop to superstition before it is too late. If you ask me, the idea of saving science from paranormal entertainment by launching a mail-in fund-raiser is so improbable that it suggests the skeptics are caught up in some wishful thinking of their own.

If the sigh cops ever try to frame me on trumped-up charges of wishful thinking, I have a good sigh alibi. The vocabulary of the alluringly unknown is incorrigibly self-indulgent, no doubt about it, so as a playful paranormalist, I have thought a lot about how the notion of wishing plays into the paranormal.

Dysbelievers are intent on getting on with their sciomachy about whether various phenomena have "evidential" bearing on the paranormal, so they fail to notice features of wishing that attentive, playful paranormalists would never miss. Playful paranormalists know, for example, that wishing is largely a matter of speech acts and that wishing is often a performative utterance in that under the appropriate, given circumstances, to say "I wish that such-and-such" is to wish it. That kind of knowledge frees nondysbelieving investigators to ask questions about conceptual connections between wishing and the paranormal that dysbelievers never think to address.

How are wishing, luck, and divination related? Good luck charms like horseshoes, rabbits' feet, and four-leaf clovers are common archetypes of superstition. In effect, they represent an automatization of wishing. What is their relationship to the popular techniques for wishing on a star, on a white horse, and so on? What about wishing contests, as between the two contending wishers in a wishbone pull, or between a little girl and the candles burning on her birthday cake? Why does recreation run as a theme through all of the above, from the "Loves me, loves me not" divination game of daisy petal plucking, to the symbolism of the gambling casino?

Wishing and its connection to the paranormal is a matter of considerable complexity. I am bringing it up here only to indicate how badly the dysbelievers have abused both psychology and the paranormal by dwelling on undecidable or meaningless pseudo-problems.

That New Psychology

Meanwhile, there are legitimate, intelligible questions about the psychology of the paranormal that are not being asked. So powerful have been the dysbelievers that they have made the study of the paranormal disreputable.

It would be very interesting to know, nevertheless, how the child's concept of the paranormal develops, or how a human being's concept of the paranormal develops from childhood into adolescence, and through adulthood into senescence. Child and adult developmental studies are an important and respected area of psychological inquiry. But the dysbelievers have seen to it that very few developmental studies of the paranormal are conducted.

At the same time, a creditable branch of psychology that has much to contribute to the study of the paranormal has been left out in the cold. Called *anomalistic psychology,* it is a legitimate scholarly specialty that catalogues and mulls over strange phenomena of the mind that usually are unknown among the general public, and often are unfamiliar to the average qualified psychologist or mental health professional.

Anomalistic psychology must be sharply distinguished from parapsychology. Parapsychology, corrupted as it is by dysbelieving, is no psychology at all, but anomalistic psychology is nondysbelieving and academically unobjectionable.

Many of the odd states of consciousness or bizarre behaviors within the purview of anomalistic psychology are rare; others are common, but not commonly recognized. All of them seem freakish or extraordinary or weird or strange, so they cover some of the same territory that the paranormal does. Sometimes, they factor in to phenomena or experiences that routinely are dubbed paranormal in the popular perception.

Playful paranormalism must be firmly grounded in the anomalies of psychology. It goes without saying that anyone who aspires to expertise about the paranormal must be thoroughly knowledgeable about hypnagogia, psychogenic amnesia, deja vu, dissociation, hallucinations, illusions, delusions, pseudologica fantastica, fugues, and depersonalization,—all peculiarities of mental functioning that are recognized by anomalistic psychology.

The field is vast, far beyond the scope of the present work, but a single example will do to illustrate the overweening importance of anomalistic psychology to the scholarly, nondysbelieving study of the paranormal.

Seeing Is Believing or Is Believing, Seeing?

Seeing faces in clouds, a visionary experience known to most children, is an example of the visual illusion known as pareidolia. It is classified as an illusion because it is created by the mind's interpreting an objectively observable, though ambiguous, stimulus—clouds, smoke, flames, ill-defined shadows, or the like—as a meaningful image.

Many visual illusions simply dissolve when one plays close attention to them. Almost everyone has been startled by what appeared to be an unknown person lurking ominously in a darkened room, only to see the figure revert harmlessly to a hat and robe dangling from a wall hook.

Pareidolia is not like that, though. Once one has made out the profile of Elvis and his mother Gladys in a cloud bank, thereafter it becomes almost impossible not to see them up there. The more intently one looks, the more the effect is accentuated. One can even point them out to others, and they will be able to see them, too, until the cloud dissipates or rolls out of sight.

Children amuse themselves by watching the figures that appear as they gaze at clouds, or at flames dancing in the fireplace, and the same perceptual process underlies several forms of divination.

Is it possible that, to reverse the old axiom, believing is seeing?

The Kahunas of Hawaii pose questions to themselves and then peer into the clouds, believing and expecting that the patterns seen there will reveal the answer they seek.

Capnomancy, or divination by smoke gazing, is still practiced among certain indigenous groups in Central America; in Medieval Europe the practice was limited exclusively to virgins or matrons.

Tea leaf reading, too, depends upon the seer's construing clusters of tea leaf fragments as meaningful pictures.

And remember that shamans in Australia used to foretell the future from the visions they glimpsed in funeral fires.

So, pareidolia provides another fine example of how childhood fun can blend visions into paranormal phenomena.

When pareidolia occurs in unfamiliar contexts, it sometimes manifests in strange, seemingly uncanny episodes that are of interest to students of the paranormal. This common perceptual illusion is the basis of a baffling type of collective visionary phenomenon that is regularly reported by the news media. When the face of Jesus is suddenly detected peering out from the wood grain of a hospital door, or He makes an appearance on the wall of an oil storage tank in the Midwest, we can be assured that pareidolia is at work. And these displays can be undeniably comical, a circumstance that does a playful paranormalist's heart good.

In recent years, unmistakable images of Jesus have shown up in the strands of a forkful of spaghetti pictured on an Atlanta billboard advertising a pizza parlor, amongst the leafy tendrils of an enormous kudzu vine covering a tree in a residential neighborhood in West Virginia, and on the face of a tortilla prepared by a New Mexico housewife. A priest dispatched by the church to the scene of this latter wonder admirably resorted to an experimental method in conducting his investigation. He cooked up batches of tortillas and was forced to concede that if you cook a lot of tortillas you see some pretty strange things.

Collective pareidolia tends to engage humanity's transcendent propensities. For example, once one or two people notice an unusual image somewhere and bring it to the attention of others, it becomes virtually impossible to persuade witnesses that the pattern has really been there all along. From the point of view of local folks long familiar with the site, it is as though the apparition has suddenly materialized out of nowhere. "I've been driving past that tank almost every day for years. If Jesus had been up there before, I would have seen Him long before now. I *know* He just appeared!"

When word about the manifestation spreads, pilgrims from afar flock to the spot. Regardless of whether they are consciously convinced of the manifestation or not, visitors usually are noticeably reverent in demeanor when beholding the image. Perhaps skeptics are hedging their bets, as it is usually wise for debunkers of the paranormal to do.

These happenings can bring some differences among the various approaches to the paranormal into clearer focus.

Parapsychologists shun these scenes because they don't measure up to laboratory conditions.

Skeptics show up to heckle and scorn the participants by demonstrating how easily they can make Jesus disappear by switching off a nearby street lamp.

Fundamentalists appear on the spot, admonishing everyone to beware of demons.

We sympathetic, playful paranormalists, however, delight in such events, for they too, reveal to us the nature of the paranormal. We are even willing to allow the possibility that collective pareidolia can bring serious and significant propensities of the human spirit into play, even a striving toward spiritual healing. Indeed, even the experience of it.

Expanding Our Considerations

What will it take for a serious, scholarly study of the ordinary paranormal to lose its illegitimacy? An even larger expansion of the context within which we are willing to consider what we have called the paranormal, to include not only anomalistic psychology (indispensable, we repeat, to anyone who is determined to face up to the paranormal in a professional and scholarly fashion), but also an awareness of the many striking curiosities of psychology, medicine, and psychiatry. Such an awareness is necessary for a scholar to be able to grasp the range, sweep, and complexity of the human mind sufficiently to master the intricacies of the paranormal dimension of consciousness. These striking curiosities include:

A host of medical conditions, too many even to be named, that can play formative roles in the paranormal.

The mystical, visionary, or auditory experiences, or behavioral quirks that can accompany delirium, partial complex epilepsy, intoxications, multiple sclerosis, Tourrette's disorder, migraine, and lots of other conditions.

Moving on to the medical specialty of psychiatry, the many little gems of psychopathology (some, but not all of them, also covered by the partially overlapping field of anomalistic psychology) that must be mastered by any scholar of the paranormal worth his or her salt. These psychiatric curiosities include the rare or unusual psychiatric syndromes (Capgras and other delusional identity disorders, de Clerambault's syndrome, Ganser syndrome, possession states, folie a deux, couvade, phantom boarder syndrome, Gaslighting, Cotard syndrome, to name a few), and the culture-bound psychiatric conditions (windigo, latah, amok, koro, for example).

There is enough room here only to outline in the briefest terms what needs to be known, and to promise to address all these outlandish psychological, medical, and psychiatric entities in a forthcoming volume, The Paranormal and the Abnormal.

We have an opportunity here, we playful paranormalists. But these are some of the things that must be done, and some of the ways in which we must expand the discussion, if anyone is to get really serious about any of this. And there is yet one more untapped arena of exploration—so often closed off or avoided by the big three discussers—that could yield a bounty of useful insights and information if looked at, at last, in a serious, scholarly manner.

11

A Treasure Chest
Waiting to Be Opened

As though all of this were not enough of a challenge for budding professional paranormalists, playful paranormalism's renunciation of dysbelieving opens another capacious field of scholarship for renewed inspection, and that is the history of the paranormal. Parapsychology once got itself together and swore off history as a source of paranormal wonder. The parapsychologists pronounced that dusty historical accounts of paranormal phenomena were not "evidential," to use one of parapsychology's favorite words. The witnesses to the historical paranormal being long-deceased, they are unavailable to give their direct testimony, so no "conclusions" about the paranormal could be drawn. The nonevidential status of the paranormal narratives of hoary historical tomes doesn't bother playful paranormalists a bit, however, because we are cognizant that not even today's freshest narratives are evidential in that dysbelievers' sense of the word.

The social history of the paranormal, so long untapped as a source of enlightenment, is overflowing with information that will expand and upgrade understanding of what the paranormal is. Reviewing the paranormal in history from a background of solid knowledge about anomalistic psychology and medical and psychiatric conditions affecting the mind can make some headway in the study of the paranormal, especially when the principle that the paranormal is play, humor, and entertainment is kept in mind. History is a showcase of long-forgotten notions about the paranormal and of colorful figures who put those alternate notions into practice. Historical works tend to validate what playful paranormalism has had to say about the paranormal.

Ancient Greece was chock-full of spectacles off the beaten track of today's paranormal. Herodotus wrote about Salmoxis, a teacher who caught on to the relevance of theatrics to the paranormal and applied that insight to evoke a posthumous apparition of . . . himself!

I myself have heard a very different account of Salmoxis' from the Greeks who live on the Hellespont and the Black Sea. According to this, he was a man, and lived in Samos, where he was a slave in the household of Pythagoras, the son of Mnesarchus. He subsequently gained his freedom, amassed a fortune, and returned to his native country of Thrace, where he found the people in great poverty and from his association with one of their more influential teachers, an insight into Ionian ideas and a more civilized way of living than was to be found in Thrace, he built himself a hall in which he used to entertain the leading men of the country with much liberality, and endeavor to teach them that neither he nor they, who were his guests, nor any of their descendants, would ever die, but would go to a place where they would live in perpetual enjoyment of every blessing. All the time he was trying to promulgate this new doctrine, he was occupied in the construction of an underground chamber, and when it was ready he entered it and disappeared from sight.

For three years he lived in this room underground, and his fellow countrymen missed him sadly, and mourned for him as if he were dead; then in the fourth year he reappeared, and in this way persuaded the Thracians that the doctrine he had taught was true.

Herodotus was unable to ascertain whether Salmoxis ever actually existed, but it is just within the range of the imagination to conceive that there could really have been such a hibernating thanato-dramatist, that he could have done it. This playfully bearish nethernaut would have built the aboveground portion of his Semblant Death theater as a facility for education and entertainment where he could dine his friends and amuse them as he lectured, in order to prepare their hearts and minds for transformation forever through a consciousness-raising drama. Perhaps he constructed his underground habitat over a gurgling spring and stocked it with chickens and torches and great vats of olives and a fine collection of venerable scrolls, and by serving a bearship down there publicly enacted a daring transgression of the inner boundaries between life and death.

What a skillful use of dramatic tension! No doubt some followed the happenings closely over a long period of time. Imagine the scenes around the sealed entrance to his den. "Is he still alive?" "How much longer will he be down there?" "How is his wife taking this?" Imagine then their astonishment when Salmoxis emerged, Lazurus-like, from his subterranean lair, a one-of-a-kind, public spectacle-demonstration of the impermanence, not of life, but of death.

Herodotus's comment that by his reappearance Salmoxis persuaded the Thracians that the doctrine he had taught was true may seem strange to the modern reader. But Herodotus grasped how and why Salmoxis's drama was psychologically and spiritually compelling. The bear man's performance was based on a masterful understanding of the psychology of bereavement: His friends missed and mourned for him "as if he were dead." Logicians may quarrel, but being there and witnessing the awesome event of Salmoxis's uncanny reemergence would indeed have been inward proof of immortality to those who collectively underwent the trauma of his social death by lengthy disappearance. The drama would have shifted the spectators' own, deeply felt, complex, inwardly perceived relationships among basic concepts of death, disappearance, bereavement, and reunion.

Modern psychology and psychiatry have verified that there are lots of visions to be seen and many revelations to be had under conditions of dark and narrow confinement. Holy people have long been known for their penchant for locking themselves into tight spaces for life, or for sitting out a few decades in caves, in order to commune with the supernatural.

And Descartes's revelations came to him, remember, when, somewhat in the manner of an old-time shaman, he shut himself up for a dark, wintry day in a little room heated by a stove.

So, if Salmoxis took any visionary voyages while he was holed up in his underground apartment, he would have arisen all the more paranormal a person for his long confinement. He would have been able to enthrall his compatriots with a new repertoire of tales of otherworldly adventure.

In the mid-1950s, a colorful canvas banner that exclaimed "See the Man Buried Alive" magnetized an eleven-year-old boy into a carnival sideshow. The boy paid twenty-five cents to be admitted into a tent, and just a few feet from its entrance he saw a big mound of freshly turned earth that was piled up not quite as high as his chest.

A metal pipe about a cubit in diameter stood straight up from the very top of the mound, sticking up about another foot higher than the heap of packed earth. By climbing up on the stepstool provided, the little boy could look down through the protruding pipe and see straight down, it seemed, about five or ten feet below, and there, recumbent in a tiny, brightly lit chamber, was the man buried alive.

The man's eyes were closed, he must have been asleep, but he was squirming restlessly. In those days, there weren't even any sigh cops to call, so the little boy figured out for himself that the pipe poking out of the ground was just one end of a periscopic arrangement of mirrors and metal tubes that terminated behind the canvas partition that hung across the rear section of the tent. But the bare fact that there would be a carnival attraction like that in 1955 is as complete a proof as is necessary of the deathless appeal of that old story about a man buried alive.

The deeper meanings of many universally recognized symbols have been garbled or left unintelligible because the dysbelievers who claim to be the experts on the paranormal have ignored the history of their subject. Oh, if the funda-Christians only knew where that winged staff encircled by serpents came from, why, they would quake when they tread into virtually any doctor's office or hospital. The caduceus had its origin in an old pagan technique for facilitating visions.

Dream incubation is the ancient practice of passing the night at a special place in the expectation of receiving a divine revelation through a dream or vision. Dream incubation was popular in ancient Egypt, Mesopotamia, Canaan, Israel, and Greece, and in Japan it survived well into the fifteenth century. Perhaps the best-known example is Solomon's visit to the hill shrine of Gibeon, where God appeared to him in a dream and, well pleased by the incubant's request, granted him the wisdom that he desired.

In those days, persons agonizing over insoluble problems could journey to a holy place in hopes that, during sleep, they would be favored with a dream by the divinity associated with the site. The dream would point to the solution of the seeker's problems.

In Greece, the rite was practiced at temples dedicated to Asklepios, a revered hero-physician king of thessaly. He was so remarkable a healer that, after his death, he was elevated to the status of a deity. Regarded as the son of Apollo, he was celebrated as the god of healing. Asklepios's symbol was the caduceus, and that is why it became the emblem of the medical profession.

If one were afflicted with an illness no conventional doctor had been able to cure, or beset by a difficulty one could no longer bear, one could journey to one of the three hundred and twenty temples of Asklepios that dotted the Greek landscape, there through dreams and visions to consult the legendary physician himself. The primary healing center of this kind was at Epidaurus, and it had adequate facilities to house and to feed the swarms of people who constantly were there awaiting their turns.

Once the time came and ritual preparations had been completed, the pilgrim entered a courtyard and slept under the stars until he or she had a specific kind of dream: Asklepios, dressed in a fur coat and with caduceus in hand, appeared and invited the incubant into the central sanctuary, the *abaton*. The abaton was an enormous building that was equipped with an impressive array of beds of roughly the same shape as those recliners that were popular during the Victorian era. They were couches, one end of which was elevated so that the head and trunk of a reclining person would be elevated above the hips and legs. This kind of bed was known as a *klini*, and the modern word clinic is derived from the term.

It was believed that Asklepios himself entered the abaton during the night, appearing as a figure in the nocturnal visions of the incubants as they reclined on the couches. This preternatural entity proffered tender concern and healing.

Grateful seekers commissioned stonecutters to inscribe the details of the patients' illnesses, their visions in the abaton, and the resulting cures on upright pillars so that others might learn of Asklepios's miracles. More than two millennia later, the clinical case studies that have survived make fascinating reading. Sometimes the spectral healer would prescribe a treatment, sometimes there would be a laying on of hands. And Asklepios had a kindly sense of humor, as is exemplified by this ancient account of a healing he brought about in the abaton.

> Euphanes, a boy of Epidaurus. Suffering from stone he slept in the temple. It seemed to him that the god stood by him and asked: "What will you give me if I cure you?" "Ten dice," he answered. The god laughed and said to him that he would cure him. When day came he walked out sound.

Time and again, the testimonials preserved at Epidaurus carefully record that the writers' visions took place "in the state between sleeping and waking," that is, that they were in a kind of reverie when Asklepios visited them. It is plausible to assume that the incubants' words referred to the hypnagogic state, a kind of halfway zone through which one passes as one is falling asleep, and that is attended with vivid imagery.

There was a vast, acoustically excellent theater at Epidaurus, too, so one can infer that plays and other entertainments took place there as well. Later, an *odeion*, an auditorium for musical performances, was built there so that music could be incorporated into the healing practices. That all this humor and entertainment was marshaled at the very spot where paranormal adventures were taking place is completely in line with sound playful paranormalist doctrine.

Playful paranormalism honors the hilarious Hellenistic writer Lucian of Samosota (117–180 A.D.) as the official humorist of the Other Side. A creative genius who was probably the greatest pre-"play and the paranormal"-ist of antiquity, he saw artistic possibilities rather than fodder for dry academic exercises in the foibles of us, the devotees of the paranormal. Lucian loved to deflate con men who preyed on the gullible by falsely claiming to have paranormal abilities or experiences. He wrote some insightful, though perhaps one-sided analyses, of the motivations of persons who promoted the paranormal.

He made fun of the bogus travel books of antiquity that described strange wonders beyond the known world. He neatly caricatured the genre in his book *A True History*, in the preface of which he exposed the fallacies of that kind of work.

> Cresias the Cnidian wrote about the land of the Indians and the regions near there, compiling things he neither saw himself nor heard from anyone's report. And Iambulus, too, recorded many marvels regarding places in the great sea; he's recognized by everyone as an inventor of lies, yet nevertheless the weave of his composition is not unpleasing. . . . But the captain of these men and chief preceptor of such foolish nonsense is Homer's Odysseus, who related to Alcinous' people the episodes of the enslavement of the winds, and the one-eyed men, and the savages, and various wildmen. . . . With many similar things that hero enchanted the provincial Phaeacians.

In the body of *A True History*, Lucian solemnly recounted his own pretended journey beyond the ends of the ocean and all the way up to the moon. After describing the many wonders he saw there, he added, "If anyone doubts what I say, let him go up there himself, and he will find out that I speak the truth."

Lucian's humor serves just as effectively to rebut a parallel fallacy into which overly eager thanatonauts sometimes lapse. Caught up in the thrill of relating their trips beyond death's door, near-death enthusiasts may try to preempt doubters by announcing, "When you die, you'll see that I'm right!" But this kind of pseudo-logic is patently unfair, and all good playful paranormalists ought to renounce it.

Lucian had a keen sense of the intrinsically comic status of the near beyond. In one of his stories, a newly deceased man arrived at the shores of the river and attempted to board Charon's boat. The oarsman wouldn't let the dead man aboard, though, because he didn't have the required fare. He decided to swim across, and he wasn't worried a bit because, "Even if I get out there in the middle and sink, it won't matter—seeing that I'm already dead."

Lucian made his living as a comic entertainer. He went on tour to read or to recite his written works before popular audiences. He knew that the paranormal is already on a comedian's side. Lucian understood that the paranormal communicates in humorologic. And his humor about the paranormal is just as funny today as it was when he wrote it almost two thousand years ago.

Creating a Context for Truly Scholarly Study

Without historical knowledge, how can we talk intelligently about the paranormal? Can any truly serious study of the subject be undertaken outside of this context?

The three ancient Greek examples are enough to indicate that social history is full of memorable characters who participated actively in the paranormal as practitioners or performers. By comparison, dysbelieving is a passive, readers' and debaters' mode of participating. The average dysbeliever-expert doesn't have a lot of working knowledge of the paranormal, compared to Salmoxis, or to the Asklepian attendants who worked at the klini-sides in the abaton. Dysbelieving "experts" lack Lucian's insight into the humorological character of discourse about the paranormal.

Dysbelieving about the paranormal is a pastime for shut-ins and stay-at-homes; it is the paranormal as seen from an armchair. Our society is caught up in what playful paranormalists categorize as a couch potato model. Viewers sit passively on a sofa and watch television panel discussions about the paranormal. There are a couple of people on the panel who describe their own, personal paranormal experiences of peri-mortal visions, apparitions of deceased, dreams that came true, or whatever. Then, two or more dysbelieving experts slug it out before the cameras, pretending to explain what the paranormal experiences mean, that is, whether or not they "prove" life after death, precognition, and so on. Viewers are supposed to make up their minds by evaluating what the panel of experients and dysbelieving experts say. Dysbeliever experts aren't expected to be able to perform the paranormal, or to be able to enable others to experience the paranormal, as ancient Greek experts were.

Playful paranormalists say, to change the study of the paranormal for the better, change the model of participation. Operating under the unific principle that the paranormal is entertainment, it is possible to symphonize anomalistic psychology, social history, and clinical know-how to enable people to have their own, firsthand paranormal experiences. Then they will be in a better position to make up their own minds about what such experiences mean. That would be to resolve a pivotal dilemma.

Many of those who study the supernatural are chronically distressed because near-death experiences, ghosts, premonitions and the like are spontaneous and unpredictable happenings that cannot be reproduced under set conditions conducive to scientific examination. So investigators are reduced to sifting through a rubble of reports made sometime after the purportedly paranormal occurrences themselves—retrospective narratives the scientific skeptics belittle as anecdotes.

If visionary reunions with the departed, peri-mortal visions, seeming foreseeings of the future, are what they purport to be, they would involve transactions between ordinary reality and what presumably would be other, alternate levels or dimensions of reality. Science has been extraordinarily successful, in part, because of its steadfast and commendable determination to confine its deliberations to this ordinary reality in which we find ourselves. However, the performing arts routinely and reliably effect transactions between ordinary reality and intriguing alternate realities. Playgoers, moviegoers, concertgoers, for example regularly are transported, still in their seats, into seemingly different realms of being. They are made to feel that they are in the midst of an entirely different order of things. So, by modeling themselves partly on the performing arts, playful paranormalists can entertain the prospect actually of reproducing experiences or phenomena that, when occurring spontaneously, often are deemed paranormal.

If that prospect could be realized, and if a particular technique for realizing it could be described in words clear enough to enable other playful paranormalists to perform an identical feat and to get the same results, that would be to inaugurate a new form of research into the paranormal. Playful paranormalists require themselves to be very careful here, however; they are not going to toss around the idea of paranormal phenomena's being reproducible in the more precise sense of the word *reproducible* that scientists mean. Playful paranormalists will not imply that theirs is a scientific enterprise. Playful paranormalists will not commit the parapsychologist's fallacy. They will not tread on legitimate scientific sensitivities by speaking lackadaisically about the possibility of the *replication* of their studies or findings, for example. Rather, playful paranormalists' concerns coincide in the prospect of *recreation* of seemingly paranormal experiences in a twofold sense—duplication plus entertainment.

Playful paranormalism is a pragmatic theory. By reading further in the historical record, we find an excellent test case for illustrating the utility and fecundity of the entertainment theory of the paranormal vis-à-vis the dysbelieving theories. History contains information sufficient to enable playful paranormalists reliably to recreate one of the most astonishing and inspiring forms of paranormal visionary experience—apparitions of the deceased.

Incredible though it may seem, in ancient Greece there were institutions known as psychomanteions, or oracles of the dead, to which people traveled to consult with the spirits of the deceased, not through the intercession of a medium, but in the course of what the seekers took to be firsthand, person-to-spirit, visionary reunions. The writings of the epic poet Homer, the historians Herodotus and Plutarch, the comic playwright Aristophanes, the geographer Strabo, the travel writer Pausanius, and other ancient authors, clearly imply that the oracles of the dead actually existed. According to the ancient authorities, seekers at the psychomanteions saw their departed relatives or friends, interacted with them, and conversed with them directly.

The most renowned of these fancifully preternatural institutions was in Thesprotia, in the far northwest corner of Greece. Strabo wrote that the oracle of the dead was situated far beneath the earth. Its entrance overlooked a large, swampy lake fed by the Acheron River.

In 1958 archeologist Sotirios Dakaris rediscovered the place. Upon excavation, the oracle of the dead turned out to be an enormous subterranean complex. There were dormitories to accommodate the travelers who came for visionary reunions and spacious living quarters for staff members, who guided apparition-seekers through the oracular process.

The resident guides were known as psychogogues. The historical record doesn't contain enough information to determine the procedures they used, but their name is suggestive. Psychogogia, literally "the leading of minds," connoted an image of flight. Originally, the word meant any kind of efficacious discourse. Ancient literary critics and philosophers used it to characterize the electrifying effect that poetry, rhetoric, and philosophical discourse could exert on listeners. It was also applied to historical and other kinds of factual writing. Later on, the geographer Eratosthenes (275–194 B.C.) redrew the boundary lines to lay claim to the prosaic uses of language for the precise purposes of science, including determining the circumference of the earth, which he did to within just a few miles of the actual figure. He argued that the essential purpose of poetic works is not to instruct but to amuse, so he narrowed the meaning of psychogogia to entertainment—a development that playful paranormalist theory could have predicted. Those bombastic busybodies, the funda-Christians, will put on their trademark smirks of smug self-satisfaction when they learn that the term has often been translated as "bewitchment."

Within the oracle of the dead on the Acheron, a long corridor led from the dormitory rooms to a maze. Negotiating the labyrinth in total darkness probably helped trigger alternate states of awareness necessary for visionary reunions. Archeologists found several sacksful of burned bits of hashish on the floor of the maze, so the seekers' consciousness was chemically augmented, too.

Deep underground, the labyrinth opened into the central feature of the facility, an apparition hallway about fifty feet long. There, archeologists found the remnants of an enormous bronze cauldron. It was surrounded by a balustrade that kept apparition-viewers from crowding too close. Apparently, visitors encircled the cauldron and looked toward it, where they saw the spirits of deceased loved ones.

Dakaris concluded that the psychogogues hid in the cauldron and acted out the roles of the deceased people that the visitors came to see. But the oracle of the dead on the Acheron was in continuous operation for at least a millennium, and it seemed to me that the people who founded Western rationality were too clever to have fallen for such an obvious trick for so long a time. I conceived a different hypothesis.

In many cultures, people used polished metal bowls, basins, and cups filled with olive oil or other liquids as speculums for mirror gazing. There is no conclusive evidence that the seekers at the oracle of the dead evoked the spirits of the deceased by gazing into the cauldron, but it is plain that the psychogogues could have known about that method. There are several lines of evidence that the ancient Greeks understood the principle that it is possible to visualize apparitions in the clear optical depths of transparent or reflective objects or liquids.

There is a mirror-gazing scene early in Homer's *The Iliad*, one of the foundation stones of Greek culture. Sitting beside the sea, Achilles saw a vision of his mother, Thetis, take form in the gray mists offshore. She emerged from the depths of the water, came onto the beach, and engaged her son in a lengthy conversation.

Several of the so-called Greek magical papyri give specific instructions for evoking spirits by gazing into metal bowls and

other vessels. These documents are collections of magical formulas and spells written in the Greek language. They were
discovered in Egypt, where the arid climate is excellent for the
preservation of scrolls. The surviving examples date from the
second century B.C. to the fifth century A.D., but religious
fanatics destroyed scrolls of this type by the cord, so we have
only a minute fraction of them today. They come from a time
when Egypt was under the influence of the Greek culture, and
scholars who have studied them are of the opinion that they
give accurate glimpses of Greek popular religious and magical
practices. Here is an example typical of the genre.

> Whenever you want to inquire about matters, take a
> bronze vessel, either a bowl or a saucer, whatever kind
> you wish. Pour water: rainwater if you are calling upon
> heavenly gods, seawater if gods of the earth, river water
> if Osiris or Sarapis, springwater if the dead. Holding the
> vessel on your knees, pour out green olive oil, bend
> over the vessel and speak the prescribed spell. And
> address whatever god you want and ask about whatev-
> er you wish, and he will reply to you and tell you about
> anything. And if he has spoken, dismiss him with the
> spell of dismissal, and you who have used this spell will
> be amazed. . . . Finally, when you have called, whomev-
> er you called will appear, god or dead man, and he will
> give an answer about anything you ask. And when you
> have learned to your satisfaction, dismiss [him] . . . as
> you say, "Depart, master, for the great god . . . wishes
> and commands this of you."

12

COMING FULL CIRCLE:
BACK TO THE SUBJECT OF LIFE
AFTER LIFE

By now it may very well have seemed that we will never return to the opening topic of this book. I have taken a long way around to come back to what, to me, is the heart of the matter, namely, those astonishing peri-mortal visionary experiences with which *Life After Life* is concerned. At the beginning of the volume at hand, though, the controversy about the near-death experience was at an impasse, partly the upshot of the stifling, hackneyed guidelines that then dictated how controversy about purportedly paranormal phenomena was to be conducted. We have come back to the starting point now in a far stronger position, having rebutted the three stale, worn-out dysbelievings and, as a bonus, having shown that it is we, the playful paranormalists, who are the true experts on the unknown!

Yes, I admit it! Again! I am a playful paranormalist. It is from that place that I have always been coming, it is where I have been residing all of these years, and it was my philosophical home well before the publication of *Life After Life*, even though the media and my former publisher and everyone else in creation worked so hard to cast me in the role of "expert" on life after death.

I was not an expert, am not now an expert, and do not expect soon to become an expert, on life after death. Certainly not if an "expert" is one who claims to know all, or at least most, of what there is to know on a subject. However, if an "expert" is one who knows that he does not know, and says that he does not know, then I am an expert—on the "unknown."

And while I want to make that very clear, I also want to clearly say that I believe I stand well outside the circle of those who know even less; those who *do* depict themselves as "expert"; those who do proclaim to have all, or most of, the answers on this subject.

As one who is decidedly not one of the big three, I believe myself to have a far more open mind on the question of life after death, and all of the other questions about the paranormal that are, of necessity, attendant to it.

My interest in the whole subject of life after death, combined with my open-mindedness, created in me a willingness to explore the topic not from a place of literalness, as do the fundamentalists, nor from a place of scientific provability, as do the skeptics, nor from a place of disparagement of anecdotal evidence, as do the detached parapsychologists, nor from any of the ancient conventions and limitations characterizing the ongoing controversy about the paranormal, but from a place of childlike willingness to explore everything playfully, but with intention to look closely and with respect at what my explorations revealed.

Allow me to give you just one example of what this mindset has produced: I said earlier that several of the so-called Greek magical papyri give specific instructions for evoking spirits by gazing into metal bowls and other vessels, and I wrote a little more about that at the end of the last chapter. In my own life, I did not simply absorb that information, and then discard it or accept it, depending on where, within my already constructed value system and beliefs, it fit in. I wanted to do more than judge this information, I wanted to evaluate it. (Of course, judging and evaluating are not nearly the same thing.) What I heard about the Greeks inspired me to attempt to recreate apparitions of the deceased by a mirror-gazing procedure.

I designed an apparition chamber, and a craftsman constructed it to my specifications. It consists of an enclosed, lightproof, soundproof, closet-sized room, the walls of which are completely black. A mirror, four feet high and four feet wide, is mounted on one wall of the room. The bottom edge of the mirror is approximately three feet above the floor.

The carpenter removed the legs from a comfortable easy chair so that it would sit low on the floor. We placed it facing the mirror, which is about three feet in front of the chair. The headrest is inclined slightly backwards so that someone sitting in the chair can relax and rest comfortably.

I placed a little lamp with a $4^1/_2$-watt bulb directly behind the chair so that its light doesn't reflect in the mirror. When the door to the room is closed and the lamp is switched on, the light diffusely illuminates the apparition chamber. From that angle, and under those conditions of illumination, someone sitting in the chair doesn't see his or her reflection. Rather, there is only a clear optical depth in the mirror.

I sought volunteer subjects from among friends who were graduate students of psychology. As word about the project spread, colleagues from the fields of psychology, medicine, and sociology contacted me and asked to participate. All subjects were bright, curious people, who were emotionally stable and interested in the study of consciousness.

Each volunteer was asked to choose one deceased loved one to attempt to see. The volunteers themselves suggested the idea of bringing to the session treasured objects that had belonged to the deceased and that the subjects poignantly associated with the departed. Since evocation of the deceased touches upon deeply personal feelings, subjects came to my research facility alone, and I conducted the evocations on a one-on-one basis. I prepared each subject in the course of a session of an hour or two, during which I asked them about the deceased loved one they wished to see. I asked very general, open-ended questions intended not for eliciting information but for getting the subjects to talk. I surmised that the more they talked, and the less I did, the likelier it was they would have visionary reunions. During our discussions, the subjects showed me the mementos they brought, and I asked them the emotional meaning of each one.

After they had talked as much as they would, I ushered them into the apparition chamber, instructing them to sit in the chair, where they would relax and gaze into the depths of the mirror. I told them I would come back in about an hour or an hour and a half. When that time elapsed, I retrieved them, escorted them into my study, and asked them to describe what, if anything, they had experienced in the apparition chamber.

I guided more than a hundred people through the evocation procedure. They included psychologists, psychiatrists, an ophthalmologist, a radiologist, social workers, businessmen and businesswomen, a fashion designer, and several authors. They shared an interest in the exploration of consciousness.

About half felt they were reunited with lost loved ones during the process. Many saw lifelike, three-dimensional visions of departed dear ones. Sometimes, they saw apparitions in the mirror, and sometimes the apparitions emerged from it. In about a third of the cases, subjects heard the voices of their lost loved ones. In almost all the other cases, subjects felt they were in mind-to-mind or soul-to-soul communion with their departed. Sometimes, there were lengthy conversational interchanges.

In nearly every instance, subjects felt a vivid sense of presence. To my great surprise, they interpreted the reunions as real events. Happily, healings took place. Subjects said the experiences helped them to move on in their grief or to resolve unfinished business.

Several psychologists in the United States and Europe set up psychomanteions, and confirmed my results. It is possible, fairly reliably, to recreate visionary reunions with the deceased, a common paranormal phenomenon.

Visionary reunions are an integral feature of many peri-mortal visions, too, so evocation of the deceased enables investigators to recreate a vital part of the near-death experience. Two of my subjects previously had near-death experiences, during which they saw departed loved ones. When asked to compare, both subjects said their visionary reunions in the psychomanteion were indistinguishable from those they experienced when they almost died.

The point I am making: it was only my willingness to know that I did not know that allowed me the space to construct and conduct such an experiment. It was only my ability to get in touch with the entertainment value of the experiment that allowed me never to become tired of it, or bored with it, through dozens of participants. Indeed, it was the entertainment value of the experiment that made it not only so much fun, but also so valuable. My refusal to dismiss the experiment as just so much "hocus-pocus," but to admit that it was hocus-pocus and then say, "Let's see what comes of this hocus-pocus," is what opened the doors for some fascinating observations, and the fascinating conclusions which they allowed me to, er . . . entertain.

Now it's time to move beyond this single example, and this single experiment. It is time to get down to the specifics of applying the principles of playful paranormalism to enhance the understanding of near-death visions. And it happens that near-death experiences know many splendid ways to entertain.

13

HAVING THE LAST LAUGH

I have sought to make three main points with this book:

The controversy about near-death experiences, and all of what we call the paranormal, has moved nowhere in the past fifty years (probably in the past several hundred) in terms of plowing new ground, producing new knowledge, or revealing ancient wisdom. This stalemate, this logjam, is the result of the "rules of engagement" surrounding any serious discussion of the paranormal in our society, rules that have limited the categories of people to whom we will listen to three:

Parapsychologists
Scientific skeptics
Religious fundamentalists

The reason the discussion has not moved forward, and has not addressed (much less answered) the questions about the paranormal that really mean something to ordinary people is that the three categories of discussers all have a vested interest in keeping the controversy going without resolution. They have managed to do this through the use of a number of devices, including limited and literal vocabulary, and a staunch refusal to look at the paranormal in any way, or from any perspective, that might prove heretical to their already entrenched points of view. In short, everyone is taking the subject too seriously, too literally, and much too narrowly to see what is really there to see, and thus to make some really new discoveries about it. In this, the big three discussers have left behind the ordinary person on the street, who is having paranormal experiences right and left (and talking about them openly and convincingly), while the so-called "experts" are proclaiming that such experiences are not possible, or are explicable as psychological aberrations, wishful thinking, or the work of the devil.

It is necessary now to open up the debate, and to include at the roundtable that category of explorers that I have chosen to call playful paranormalists—for the time has come to look at things a new way, to stop taking everything so seriously, and, in fact, to consider the possibility that the very reason that ordinary people find the subject of the paranormal so continually fascinating is precisely because they do not take it seriously, but, rather, find the whole topic eminently entertaining—a grand diversion. Indeed, part of what the public finds to be the most entertaining about the paranormal are the ideas that the paranormal suggests, and the thought that they may be true! Playful paranormalists hold that what begins as extraordinary entertainment could end as extraordinary revelation, if we would just allow the show to go on, letting it show us whatever it may have to show us (if anything) about what the big show is really all about.

This, of course, is where I have been coming from all along, and no one was more aghast than I to discover that, as a result of the extraordinary and completely surprising success of my book *Life After Life,* the public at large had decided that I, in fact, was now one of the world's leading "experts" on peri-mortal realities.

I mean, here I was, hypothesizing with all the rest of the world about what might or might not be true about life after death, sharing the utterly fascinating anecdotal data I had come up with, and exploring the possible conclusions to which they might lead us. Suddenly, I found my own joyful explorations set in stone. They had become the Truth, and I had become the Expert. And any effort on my part to expand on the exploration, or to keep the questions open, was met with a lot of opposition. Nobody wanted to hear it. I had arrived at my conclusions, and that was that.

But that wasn't that. I never meant for the exploration of this subject to end with my thesis, but to *begin*. At last, I thought, we are going to have a serious, scholarly study of this anecdotal data I have brought to the public's attention in such a dramatic (and thus, entertaining) way.

As a lover of topics paranormal for decades, I enjoyed these original explorations immensely. I mean, to put it simply, they were fun.

All scientists, if they are honest, will tell you that this is what has driven every real discovery. There is a fire in the belly, a burning passion deep inside of every scientist, theorist, or explorer of any kind. That passion is what is *fun*. It is like any other passion. Passion is fun, exploded. Magnified. Intensified to such a degree that it rules the moment, and, in so doing, often produces miracles. Sometimes they may be miracles of love. Sometimes, miracles of discovery. Sometimes the miracle of remembrance of a long-forgotten wisdom. But always a miracle, and never anything boring. Passion cannot produce boredom. Not for the person who is experiencing the passion. It is impossible. The two are mutually exclusive.

Since all passion is fun, and all fun is entertaining, I have no doubt at all that the reason I have had such an intense interest in the paranormal for so many years is that my mind has found the entire topic wonderfully entertaining.

What Will Happen If We Can All Look at It This Way

Now if we can *all* look at it that way, we might actually join forces and discover something new. We might open a new window onto the alluringly unknown, and find on the winds of some wonderfully fresh air a wonderfully fresh idea that produces a wonderfully fresh hypothesis that results in a wonderfully fresh approach to wonderfully fresh explorations leading to wonderfully fresh knowledge. We might just wind up changing a little of that unknown into that which is known, and expanding, at long last, our awareness and our understanding of the mysteries to which our collective human soul has been drawn from the beginning of time.

Among them, there has been no more alluring mystery than the question of what happens to us after what we are wont to call death. So far, the closest we have been able to come to answering that question has been to explore what occurs in the so-called *near*-death experiences of others.

Regretfully, we have done so quite seriously, using limited vocabularies and constricted ground rules for that exploration (including the elimination of any data that is not judged to be psychologically sound, scientifically proven, and supported by traditional religious teaching. And, mind you, it has to meet the criteria of *all three,* not merely one or the other, or even two out of three), with the result that we have produced no answers at all.

I really thought that my book *Life After Life* would serve as a stimulus to break out in new directions on this subject, but all it really did was cause the big three to dig in deeper, refusing to budge from their entrenched understandings and the positions those understandings required them to take. The book did receive enormously widespread *public* support, and its acceptance by ordinary people (as opposed to the "experts") said something about who the real experts are, and who really knows what's going on and what's true, or at least what *could* be true, about the paranormal.

Now I'm inviting all those regular, ordinary people who have stood by and watched (no doubt as mystified as was I) as the "experts" remained glued over the past twenty-five years to their rigid and immobile positions regarding life after death (the miles-high pile of anecdotal evidence to the contrary notwithstanding), to take things into their own hands. It is time for us—all of us who are willing to say that we do *not* know the truth—to push the envelope, to reengage the question, and to challenge those discussers who claim that they *do.* It is time for us to say to them, "Yes, but what *if?*" It is time for us to entertain the notion that what we have been hearing from thousands of people anecdotally might very well be not simply entertaining, but ultimately revealing.

In short, it is time for us to have the last laugh.

So many of those who call themselves experts of the paranormal, or on whom we have bestowed a certain moral or scientific authority in this regard, will not even listen to what those who claim to have had near-death experiences have to say.

Too many priests, ministers, and rabbis shush people who have "come back" with such reports. Too many psychologists and psychiatrists take the reports very seriously indeed—as evidence of some deep psychosis, or, at the least, the need for some calming medication. And too many skeptics set out with such verbal and emotional brutality to debunk such honestly given reports that the original tellers wish they'd never opened their mouths.

This is what happens when everyone insists on taking all this so seriously.

Still, all of that notwithstanding, we, the ordinary people of the world, continue to listen to (and even to encourage, for they are vastly entertaining) such reports, for we are titillated, inspired, rejuvenated, encouraged, and deeply enlivened by the possibility that they *might* be true.

The human written record reveals the near-death experience to be an exceedingly ancient phenomenon, but it has come into its own during our era as the result of a complicated interaction among a number of factors, not the least of which is technology.

During the past few decades, there have been advances in cardiopulmonary resuscitation that were undreamed of a century ago. Equipment and techniques have been developed that enable physicians routinely to bring patients back from a condition that only a few decades ago would have been known as death, with the surprising consequence that netherworld journeys have become everyday occurrences.

And now, a conundrum: parallel remarks could be made, mutatis mutandis, about other exciting modern advances—trips to the moon, for example. The latter have come to seem humdrum (people are so bored by them that NASA cannot even get space shots televised anymore, the networks begging off because, in spite of their historical significance, they bring horrible ratings!), but near-death experiences, now out in the open for two decades, continue to fascinate. In fact, the level of interest in the phenomenon seems to be on the increase. Why is this so?

It is precisely because we are so entertained by it. And until we can accept the paranormal as entertainment, lightening up a little bit about it, we will never be able to accept what it may have to show us as truth at any later date.

If we had not been so richly entertained over the years by films such as *E.T., Cocoon,* and others, do you think we would stand a chance of ever calmly accepting the truth about life on other planets?

If we had not been stimulated by such books as *The Celestine Prophecy* and *Conversations with God,* do you think we would stand a chance of ever calmly accepting the truth about life on *this* planet?

And if we had not been captivated by the sayings of Confucius, the parables of Jesus, or the stories of any of our greatest teachers (all of whom understood full well that they must entertain first, if they are to enlighten), do you think we would stand a chance of ever calmly accepting the truth about ourselves, and our very nature?

It is at this point that the principles of playful paranormalism can effectively be brought to bear. The question, "What is the basis of the continuing appeal of the near-death experience?" has now been answered. The answer, again, is: We are entertained by it.

That, my friends, is the last laugh. Because everyone has been taking this life-after-death and this paranormal stuff so seriously. And it is that very seriousness that has precluded any possibility of new discovery—which is one of the grandest joys (and thus, the greatest entertainments) of all.

There is something very funny about that. I mean, it is so wickedly self-defeating that it is almost funny in its implications.

Could All This Be a Mixed Blessing?

Playful paranormalists enjoy challenges. We are itching to get quickly to the seemingly difficult cases for our entertainment theory. Specifically, in applying the humorological concept of the paranormal to the case of peri-mortal visions, some apparent objections or counterexamples come up that suggest that the vast entertainment appeal of the near-death experience is a mixed blessing.

There are a couple of worrisome, irksome "dysapplications" of peri-mortal visionary experiences as popular diversion or entertainment. They are another reason, paradoxically, why near-death experiences need to be put into a humorous perspective, for both dysapplications involve taking something too seriously.

A good sense of humor is the best tool a playful paranormalist can use to dispense with the numb-minded conservatism about peri-mortal visionary experiences that, incredibly, has set in so quickly among lots of folks who devote themselves to the subject as a pastime. Those fans want all their near-death experience entertainment fare to be just as they are used to enjoying it. They want more of the same old, same old, and they want more and more of it. An appreciable number of them have bunched themselves together into a special-interest hobby club, the International Association for Near-Death Studies, or IANDS, and there are some good things about that organization. It offers supportive group settings for the benefit of near-death experients and their families who are dealing with emotional aftereffects. The association sponsors a fine journal that has been publishing articles by specialists in many diverse disciplines, representing a broad spectrum of opinions, for more than a decade, and the editor takes no party line on near-death experiences.

But on the down side, passionate IANDSists speak an annoying jargon of their own. The phrase "near-death experience" is awkward-sounding enough as it is. But their familiarizing it by shortening it to "NDE" makes it sound uglier, in my estimation. The abbreviation grates even harder on the nerves. Why is it that avid IANDSites always say "experiencers" as they do, and never soften their vocabulary with any "experients"?

If you ask me, some of them have gotten hung up on NDEs. They are too touchy about someone going outside the bounds of what they think they already know about the subject.

I've been persona non grata with the group since 1989, the last time they asked me to speak to their convention. I thought they wanted to hear about the latest wrinkles in my studies of near-death experiences and related, extraordinary states of consciousness, so I presented my new research on mirror visions. It turned out they had wanted to rehear the same old stuff—again! Many members concluded I had gone off the deep end.

An IANDS official I haven't even met, a self-certified expert on NDEs, felt she knew me well enough to refer to me by my first name when she commented in a newspaper article about my study of the evocation of the deceased. A woman named Nurse Kookoran, or something sounding like that, was quoted as saying, "Raymond is off on a tangent." As a good obsessive, I will admit to circumstantiality, but tangentiality is a different matter entirely. I became interested in the oracles of the dead in 1962, in near-death experiences in 1965!

Recently, an old friend of mine, a founding member of IANDS, said that at the last meeting he attended there was a lot of singing going on, and he was left with the impression of a religious revival. Take that sort of thing any further and you start running the risk of creating an ideology about near- death experiences. Then you're really in trouble.

Playful paranormalism is a good antidote for anyone who takes NDEism seriously, the IANDS type or any other.

Who Ordinary People Listen to about Near-Death Experiences—And Why

Yet, who are ordinary people—people not caught up in beginning ideologies, or movements, or the conventions and positions of the big three discussers—listening to?

Well, in recent times the complex, fascinative, and amusive dynamics of near-death experiences have set the stage for their exploitation in the entertainment media. So, it was predictable that popular demand for tidings from the near beyond would give rise to a new breed of performers I dub the NDEntertainers. Of course, they do not see themselves a "performers," but rather, as "informers"—people bringing information to others. But as I have noted before, there is a good performer in all effective informers. There's nothing wrong with that—if it is not taken too far.

And so, lately, we have seen folks who go on tour to recount their own, personal near-death experiences before live audiences. As they travel, these NDEntertaining NDEntre-preneurs sell their books and tapes—but no tee shirts yet. Tee shirts might be going too far. . . .

Two NDEntertainers in particular have scored big hits—Betty Eadie, author of *Embraced by the Light,* and Dannion Brinkley, who told his story to journalist Paul Perry, who skillfully crafted it into *Saved by the Light.* The NDEntertainers make an excellent stalking-horse for illustrating some of the principles of playful paranormalism, for the books and the performances of these New Age thanatothespians invite analyses somewhat along the lines of those that literary or theater critics offer about works of fiction or dramatic productions. I must admit that while I find value in using entertainment as an attention-getting tool, a literary-style criticism of the public presentations of some of the speakers now on tour brings to light some troubling contradictions inherent in that kind of NDEnterprise.

Both Betty and Dannion borrow heavily from the techniques of the performing arts to get their messages across. Betty even wears an eye-catching costume, a fancy, fringed dress with a touch of Native American style. But I have known Dannion a lot longer, so I am in a better position to offer a commentary on his monodramatic extravaganza.

I met Dannion in 1976, several months after he barely survived being struck by lightning. He told me that while he had been on the verge of death, he entered a realm of light and found himself in the company of luminescent beings. He said these beings had shown him a series of encapsulated visions that he described almost as though they had been film clips. He had been given to understand that they were visual representations of events that were to take place in the future.

Many prophets seem to foresee mostly drastic kinds of unpleasantness, and the majority of Dannion's foreseeings were the typical soothsayer-fare—looming famine, war, economic depression, societal disarray.

In the mid-1970s, when I first heard these foretellings, I was smug. As an avid, in-depth follower of current events, I felt sure the world was in for a big shake-up, a conclusion I based on simple extrapolation from the bad news of those days—the nuclear arms race, rampant poverty in the third world, carelessness about the environment, and burgeoning overpopulation—not on psychic forewarnings. I also knew enough about psychiatry to perceive that most Americans were hiding their heads in the sand about global developments. And I had heard several other near-death experients recite their own awesome, end-time visions of gloom and doom that were parallel to Dannion's. I surmised that sometimes, when people realized that they were on the verge of death, their defensive structures collapsed and their thoughts raced ahead from what was then the state of world affairs to make the likely inference: a worldwide calamity was in the offing.

Subsequently, however, I admit I have been a bit unsettled by the uncanny accuracy of some of those experients' forecasts. In 1975, my friend Vi Horton correctly foretold (from her near-death vision) the exact year, nature, and outcome of the revolution in South Africa. And in April 1976 Dannion told me that in his vision he had foreseen that in 1990 there would be a breakdown of the Soviet Union and that there would be food riots there. I recall that incident so vividly because what he said struck me as silly and absurd; I took his seriousness about the pronouncement as evidence that the bolt of electricity had disrupted his brain circuitry. Imagine my surprise fourteen years later when the event transpired just as he had forespoken it. There have been many other instances, too, when he issued predictions that seemed totally off the wall at the time, only to be fulfilled later with chilling precision.

Then I must go on immediately to add that I have seen and heard him pronounce many other prophecies, detailing even the exact day, month, or year of their forthcoming, and all in the same preemptory voice and manner of all-confident authority, that never did materialize as he said they would.

Not only that, but he has continued to prophesize ever since his near-death experience took place in September 1975 because he believes that his close call with death empowered him to read minds and to peer into the future. And his display of mind reading is among the best and most convincing I have ever witnessed. Time after time, I have seen folks' jaws drop, or tears well up in their eyes, as Dannion, a total stranger to them, correctly rattles off the details of their personal circumstances, even their deep inner secrets.

For years, I have been baffled by his amazing talent for seeming to know things about others that he seemingly would have no way of knowing. That is why I encouraged him to get his story into print. I introduced him to the persons who arranged for its publication.

But I had envisioned a different presentation; for a long time, I have wanted to see Dannion in a face-off with the Amazing Randi or other sigh cop, such as Dr. Ray Hyman, a psychologist who specializes in putting claims of telepathic powers to the test. I still hope that some day such a confrontation will come to pass. Since the release of his book, though, a couple of parapsychologically minded investigators have assessed Dannion's skills, and they profess to be as perplexed by him as I am.

Whatever the eventual outcome of the wrangling about Dannion among parapsychologists, sigh cops and funda-Christians, however, it won't make any difference to the many admirers and fans who have gathered around him. They will continue to believe he can read minds and foresee the future. Nor is Dannion ever bothered for a minute by any of his mis-foreseeings, for when prophecies fail, fresh ones soon are heard tripping from his tongue to replace the worn-out ones.

Playful paranormalists can give a much better formulation of the walking conundrum that is Dannion Brinkley than is likely to come out of any dysbeliever battles. What has always interested me most about Dannion's tale is not his near-death experience per se, since it is one of a multitude of similar ones, but, rather, its flashy accouterments. He captivates others by dressing up his account in the trappings of a charismatic, bedazzling, and enmazing personality. He is an enlightening example of a kind of person who has been of great importance in the history of the paranormal, namely, the individual who is able to interweave several popular strands of paranormal mythology into one life story.

Quite apart from his near-death experience, his prophecies, and his mind-reading, Dannion represents a confluence of a number of distinct themes that historically always have found willing audiences among the seekers of paranormal pleasure.

Examining these themes closely brings us a good insight into not only *who* people listen to about the paranormal, but why.

The Common Denominators

First, there is the matter of the lightning. Then there is the item about a bed. Both lightning and beds have figured predominantly for centuries in the best traditions of the paranormal.

As I've already indicated, Dannion's peri-mortal adventure began in a flesh-sizzling flash of lightning, and that by itself was enough to dynamize his tale with paranormal meaning, because for almost the whole of human history, lightning has been interpreted as a supernatural manifestation, and no one is impervious to its holdover paranormal symbolism.

Dannion's claim that a bolt of lightning endowed him with inexplicable talents is by no means unique. Throughout the world, especially in tribal cultures, there is a folk belief that those who walk the earth after being struck by lightning have paranormal abilities. In some traditions, practitioners who are initiated into their vocation in this way are respected as the most powerful of all shamans.

Ethnologist Holger Kalweit recorded the stories of three lightning shamans he interviewed in Peru, and he summarized stories he gathered from the literature about several electrified practitioners from other cultures.

Wolf Head, a Blackfoot medicine man, was the most intriguing lightning shaman on record. During his near-death vision, he first met Boy Thunder, a spirit being who for many years thereafter repeatedly visited Wolf Head in dreams and taught him how to be a great shaman. When he appeared in the shaman's dreams, Boy Thunder's favorite trick was to teach Wolf Head extraordinary talents or skills that the medicine man had no earthly training or education to account for.

One morning, Wolf Head woke up with the abilities of a gifted sculptor. He chiseled two full-sized busts in stone that were exact likenesses of Queen Victoria and King Edward. The anomalous artist had seen the portrait of his subjects on a medallion.

Another time, Boy Thunder taught Wolf Head how to be an excellent mining engineer overnight. The next morning, Wolf Head was off to the coal mines, where he presented a design for an entire coal mining operation. Government authorities scratched their heads and allowed that it was the best mining plan they had ever seen.

Human personality is a formative influence on the social history of the paranormal. So little of what can be said about the paranormal is concretely verifiable, that *how* it is said assumes major importance. This is a point that I have been making through this book.

I have brought up Dannion Brinkley because Dannion's saga is a case in point. His story is told with an inscrutable, idiosyncratic use of language that is inseparable from his charismatic personality style. In other words, he certainly has a dramatic flair. In addition, he is using (by chance, it would seem) at least two storytelling imageries—lightening and a bed (more about which later), which appear historically in tales of the paranormal. Finally, his *style* of storytelling is important to this analysis.

Dannion is a huge, muscular man, and he is charmingly overbearing. He can easily dominate conversations, and loves to be the center of everyone's attention. He holds listeners spellbound, on the edge of their seats, but as long as I have known him, I have never been able to track his train of thought. He speaks in a rapid-fire manner that makes it impossible for all but the quickest to get a word in edgewise. His inimitable manner of oration is a word-blizzard.

A respected Cambridge scholar wrote a tidy hypotyposis of the count de St. Germain that perfectly captures Dannion's style. According to E. M. Butler, the count "cut a dazzling figure and mystified everyone by his incognito, by dropping mysterious hints, by refusing to commit himself to the possession of powers which he nevertheless seemed to be exercising before their eyes, and by his indecipherable personality."

Now, for the bed part.

Dannion claims that during his near-death experience, otherworldly beings showed him a design for an electronic bed with healing powers. They instructed him to build this device and to install it in his healing centers. I have seen several models of this bed from beyond. They are comfortable recliners with built-in headsets that play tape-recorded music through the body by bone conduction. They induce a mellow, drifty state of relaxation. When I tried one of the beds, I found its effects indistinguishable from hypnagogia.

All that aside, Dannion's story about a supernatural settee interests me because it illustrates a bedrock principle of playful paranormalism: It replays the same old favorites again and again over the centuries, the same stock characters show up in slightly different situations, but, overall, the paranormal manages in every succeeding season to make its familiar dramas seem new and exciting.

Viewed historically, the paranormal performs somewhat like a repertory theater. For instance, the tale of "an uncanny man with a mysterious couch" is deeply embedded in the history of paranormal and other periparanormal amusements. The particulars of saints' sofas or of holy men's mats often take on significance in their life stories.

Solomon slept in a magical bed aflutter on every side with angels. Moses was set afloat in a crib woven from reeds. The infant Jesus slumbered in a manger. Then there are the Indian fakirs' hystrichomorphic cots and Asklepios's klini.

Asklepios really started something with his healing beds. Asclepiades of Bithnyia, who practiced medicine in Rome in the second century A.D., invented a huge mechanical cradle to rock patients back to health. Dr. James Graham (1745–1794), whom detractors crowned "the emperor of quacks," operated the Grand Temple of Health in London. The main attraction there was his Celestial Bed, a massive, domed contraption with almost a ton of magnets in its innards. The whole thing vibrated, and perfume sprayers in the top puffed the air full of fragrant mists. It cost a tidy sum to spend the night inside, but barren couples willingly paid, because Dr. Graham guaranteed they would conceive. Sigmund Freud is another eccentric male personage who became famous for a healing couch.

In the higher-class dens, beautiful, ornate opium beds gave periparanormalizing "poppynauts" a better view of

Xanudu. Odd bedmen have made it big in recent weird news columns, too. There has been a spate of stories about men afflicted with the Oblomov syndrome, a bizarre illness that has not yet been categorized in textbooks of anomalistic psychology or psychiatry. People with this malady confine themselves to bed without a doctor's excuse, ordered to rest by inner physicians. Sometimes they gain so much weight they can't get up by themselves. There have been several startling news reports of men weighing half a ton or more who had to be hoisted out of their houses to be transported to hospitals for emergency medical care. One was forklifted onto a flatbed truck; another was carried on a stretcher made for a small whale.

It makes sense that beds would be thought of as transition points between realms or as jumping-off places for otherworldly journeys. Even in their familiar, nightly use, beds are where people slumber away into the land of Nod. The dying often see glorious visions of the beyond from their deathbeds. The idea of beds as transition places accounts for their popularity in paranormal and other periparanormal amusements.

To sum up, Dannion Brinkley's story appeals because it ties so many colorful threads of popular paranormality together into one entertainment package.

I want to make it clear that I am writing in the abstract, and that, personally, I find Betty and Dannion to be lovable and endearing people who do good things for others. I understand, for example, that Dannion recruits volunteers for hospice during his dramatic and exciting talks with large audiences, and gets quite a few of them. I don't question either of their motives for a second. I am merely pointing out here what makes them listened to.

On balance, I expect, NDEntertainment and NDEism will prove to be more a helpful than a harmless development. They will be kept in check by the medical technology that ensures a continuing stream of new arrivals back from round trips to the near hereafter. The high incidence and high prevalence of near-death experiences are a corrective to any possible NDExcesses of NDEists or NDEntertainers.

The very best person from whom to hear the details of a near-death experience is always a close relative, a sage, grounded, experienced, sensitive person of long personal acquaintance. Almost everyone knows someone who has had a near-death experience, and that has afforded tens of millions of people the opportunity to hear the story firsthand from a beloved other person long known and long trusted—a wise Aunt Pearl, a dear grandmother or grandfather, a respected close friend. By now, that is probably as large a factor as any other in why so many people, lay or professional, dysbelievers about the paranormal or not, have become aware of the actual occurrence of these life-changing episodes.

Hearing the story directly from a good, solid, honest person with whom one has already been long and personally acquainted brings the near-death experience home in its most wondrous immediacy this side of the near beyond.

Much of what most folks' wisest loved ones have to say about their own visits to the near hereafter is soothing, loving, and cheerful in spirit. It is easy to appreciate the amusement value of happy, comforting near-death experiences.

But What about Reports of Distressing Near-Death Experiences?

Distressing peri-mortal visions have been reported, too, however, and to a beginning playful paranormalist, they might seem difficult to explain by the entertainment theory. Just you wait, though. You'll see the entertainment value of even these reports.

Particular component elements of the near-death experience may have their own characteristic amusive appeal. A few near-death experients describe a gray zone, a realm sandwiched in somewhere between their leaving their physical bodies and their entering into a comforting light of joyful love that is at the end of a dark tunnel. These experients say they glimpse this ashen dimension as they proceed through a tunnel, or in the moment before they enter the tunnel.

To the NDExperients zipping through that dreary plane, its astral occupants appear to be lost in a fog of earthly fixations. It is an experience like taking the ghost train ride at Disney World.

There are many dulled, gray spirits in there who seem unable to surrender their attachments to the physical world. These shadowy souls seem perpetually to be going through the motions of earthly existence, endlessly repeating a worldly action in an obsessive manner. They repetitively are reliving a lamentable error of their past lives, or they are so absorbed in one governing desire, and they can think of nothing else but how to satisfy it.

Dr. George Ritchie, a Virginia psychiatrist who is the first person I ever heard recount a near-death experience, related several unforgettable vignettes about the occupants of that foggy astral region. His impression of these misty specters was that "they can't progress on the other side because their god's still living here."

Dr. Ritchie said that during his apparent death from double lobar pneumonia, Christ conducted him on a sort of guided tour of several realms of the afterlife, including the gray zone. Dr. Ritchie related that at one point he was able to see into the everyday realm of human existence, and there he saw an ordinary man walking along a street. A dulled, shadowy figure, the spirit of a woman Dr. Ritchie gathered had been the man's mother while she was alive, hovered above him, following him as he walked, still trying to tell him what to do.

In another place, Dr. Ritchie was able to see into an ordinary bar in the physical world, somewhere in a large city he did not recognize. He saw ordinary humans milling about in the bar, but in addition there were other, apparently deceased patrons, gray phantoms flitting in and out among the ordinary humans. Occasionally, one of these discarnate entities would reach for a bottle of alcohol sitting on a table, but the specter's hands would slip through the bottle as though they were grasping at air. Dr. Ritchie surmised these sad souls were people who had been alcoholics while alive and who, even in their departed condition, were unable to let go of the habit.

The NDExperients who have described this realm suggest its astral inmates do not fully realize they are dead, so they are attempting to continue the rhythms of everyday existence into eternity. These shadowfolk seem timebound and deadlocked, intent on endlessly repeating an earthly hang-up forever and ever.

They are in a pretty dreadful situation, it is true, but Dr. Ritchie also saw enlightened beings moving, saintlike, in and out among the gray spirits, trying to rescue them. That must mean there is hope even in the drab region.

There is no denying the entertainment appeal of tales of this kind. Indeed, this playful paranormalist prides himself in having made an observation about these grayfolk that no one seems to have picked up on before. This detail of some near-death experiences is identical to a kind of Greek myth familiar to almost everyone—the myths of Sisyphus or of Tantalus, for example. Sisyphus was condemned in the afterlife eternally and laboriously to roll a big boulder all the way to the top of a high, steep hill, only to have it get away from him and roll all the way back down the slope, whereupon he would have to begin his labor all over at the bottom again. This endless Sisyphus-cycle of aspiration, spirited attempt, a moment of seeming success, then a sad reversal of fortune is reminiscent of the plight of the gray spirits NDExperients see laboring against insurmountable obstacles.

Tantalus's fate in the beyond was essentially the same as that of the astral alcohol abusers Dr. Ritchie described. Tantalus eternally saw food and drink immediately in front of him, but every time he reached for it, it would recede away from him and elude his grasp.

Another well-known Greek myth of this type is the story of the water carriers in Hades, poor phantoms who perpetually had to lug water in large, leaky jars. The water carriers filled the jars at a spring in the afterlife zone, but by the time they reached their destination, every drop had trickled out.

These Greek myths often are cited as allegories of earthly life, but it is not widely known that the surviving accounts of some of them derive from the reports of Greek temporary visitants to the near beyond. Our forbears in that wondrous ancient society were well aware of the strange, gloomy intermediate zone that still is sometimes reported by survivors of cardiac arrest. Plutarch wrote a hauntingly evocative description of that dim and misty halfway house of eternity: "There is nothing in that realm except a sort of unending shadow, and a gnawing dream full of yearnings that never will be satisfied."

So, a strange, enmisted twilight zone of endless frustration has been a common feature of near-death experiences and related phenomena for as long as we have records.

We humans seem to have an insatiable appetite for captivating stories of phantoms suspended in an eerily earthlike eternity. These fascinating dimpeople are disembodied, but they are not yet freed from mundane time. They behave as though there had been a grave malfunction at the moment of death; a playful paranormalist might speculate that perhaps, when they died, they got out of their bodies on the wrong side.

At any rate, this particular element of the near-death experience appeals because it taps into a profound human fascination with the notion of laboring in vain. The idea of futile toil that shows up in some peri-mortal visions also is brought alive in a host of picturesque expressions of ordinary language: to tilt at windmills, to lash the waves, to beat the air, to sow the sand, to bay at the moon, to waste one's breath, to preach to the winds, to flog a dead horse, to roll the stone of Sisyphus, to milk a ram, to pour water into a sieve, to milk a ram into a sieve, to hold a penny candle up to the sun, to look for a needle in a haystack, to go on a wild goose chase, to try to get blood from a turnip, to be on a treadmill, to be in a squirrel cage, to go around like a horse in a mill, to be in a rut, to talk to a wall.

How the Fundamentalists Have Got It Figured

The funda-Christians who study peri-mortal visions specialize in dredging up as many lurid stories as they can of people who suffered horrific torments in hell when they almost died. The fundamentalist experts rejoice and slap each other on their backs every time they find a new case of a hellish, funda-Christian near-death experience.

Those vinegarish old fundamentalists probably think the gray zone is just a Satanic ploy, too. I'll bet they imagine it is just another honeyed paranormal illusion their own favorite denizen of the near beyond manufactured to lull us unsuspecting freethinkers into a false sense of security. Deep in their fundaments, some funda-Christians no doubt suspect the devil of dreaming up the gray area to mislead us nonsubscribers to their beliefs. Satan may want those of us who don't go for funda-Christian ideology to think punishment in the afterlife is just a piece of cake, that it is nothing much at all compared to the far more horrific torments that funda-Christian authorities on near-death experiences enjoy writing and lecturing about.

Fundamentalist NDEnthusiasts tingle with fiendish delight when they read about any infernal near-death experiences, because the hellish ones fit best with their Satanology. The greater quantity of overwhelming pain a critically ill person endures during a hellish near-death experience, the better it serves the purpose of funda-Christian NDExpertise. The heavier laden a resuscitant's tale is with hair-raising details of wrenching, stabbing, piercing, shooting, gnawing, grinding, aching, burning, crushing, throbbing, cramping, stinging, smarting, harrowing pain, the happier funda-Christian NDExperts are to hear about it.

In the best, most terrifying, funda-Christian, hellish near-death experiences, the accursed resuscitants' pain would be acute and chronic, unremitting and ever intensifying, sharp and dull, fulgurant and lancinating, overwhelming and unbearable. The funda-Christian, hellish near-death experiences that moan and groan in the scariest, most extreme pangs of agony score highest on the Ravings scale.

We playful paranormalists can just see the fundamentalists now, recoiling in horror at the very idea that, related as paranormal phenomena, near-death experiences are entertainment.

"What about hellish near-death experiences?" each blustery Bible-bully will sputter with a sneer. "Is hell just fun and games, too?"

But they don't know their funda-Christian history very well, because the early Church held that hell was exactly that—entertainment!

It was a tenet of the faith that a significant portion of the joy that awaited the saved in heaven would consist of the pleasure of viewing the denizens of hell being tormented below. Jolly old Tertullian could hardly wait for the gala endtime show to begin. He felt sure it was going to be a barrel of fun.

What a panorama of spectacle on that day! Which sight shall I turn to first to laugh and applaud? Mighty kings whose ascent to heaven used to be announced publicly groaning now in the depths with Jupiter himself who used to witness that ascent? Governors who persecuted the name of the Lord melting in flames fiercer than those they kindled for brave Christians? Wise philosophers, blushing before their students as they burn together, the followers to whom they taught that the world is no concern of God's, whom they assured that either they had no souls at all or that what souls they had would never return to their former bodies? Poets, trembling not before the judgement seat of Rhadamanthus or of Minos, but of Christ—a surprise? Tragic actors bellowing in their own melodramas should be worth hearing! Comedians skipping in the fire will be worth praise! These are things of greater delight, I believe, than a circus, both kinds of theater, and any stadium.

The same sweet sentiments of vengeful consolation were expressed by St. John Chrysostom (345–407 A.D.), an early church father who was archbishop of Constantinople. His words are further proof of how closely funda-Christians' attitudes toward hilarity parallel their positions on the paranormal.

To laugh, to speak jocosely, does not seem an acknowledged sin, but it leads to acknowledged sin. Thus laughter often gives birth to foul discourse, and foul discourse to actions still more foul. Often from words and laughter proceed railing and insult; and from railing, and insult, blows and wounds; and from blows and wounds, slaughter and murder. If, then, thou wouldst take good counsel for thyself, avoid not merely foul words, and foul deeds, or blows, and wounds, and murders, but unseasonable laughter, itself. . . . Suppose some persons laugh. Do thou on the other hand weep for their transgressions. Many also once laughed at Noah whilst he was preparing the ark; but when the flood came, he laughed at them; or rather, the just man never laughed at them at all, but wept and bewailed.

When therefore thou seest persons laughing, reflect that those teeth, that grin now, will one day have to sustain that most dreadful wailing and gnashing, and that they will remember this same laugh on That Day whilst they are grinding and gnashing. Then thou too shalt remember this laugh.

Accounts of hellish near-death experiences give today's funda-Christians a similarly pleasurable foretaste of the satisfaction they will have knowing all us troublesome nonconformers are thrashing about in pain in the afterlife for not subscribing to God's and their ideology.

Some fundamentalists get their jollies from grisly tales of other people being hideously scourged and gruesomely basted, and it tickles them all the pinker if the agonizing other people are homosexuals, or Hindus, or Buddhists or Mormons or dabsters in the occult, or atheists.

Taking pleasure in contemplating other people's agony is known as sadism. Fundamentalists don't feel in the least embarrassed about indulging in that particular form of perversion, however, nor should they. Everyone has some sadistic tendencies; it's a part of being human. But openly flaunting sadistic tendencies isn't as socially acceptable now as it was when Tertullian and St. John Chrysostom wrote. Today's fundamentalists disguise their fantasies of revenge as ideology.

Yet it is their entertainment appeal that is the basis of the popularity of books about fundamentalist, hellish near-death experiences. Someone who assents to the unific principle of playful paranormalism is in a good position to appreciate the uncanny parallels between funda-Christian literature about infernal peri-mortal visions and the genre of horror fiction—the literary and the pulp varieties. Dysbelievers read the texts of the paranormal differently, depending upon the types of literature they prefer. Parapsychologists are fond of comedy. Scientific skeptics favor crime drama and social satire. Funda-Christians like horror stories. These are differences in aesthetic preferences.

In the United States, the horror genre of literature can be traced directly back to Puritan preoccupations. "Men need to be terrified . . .," one Puritan preacher wrote, "that they may be converted." Likewise, one prominent funda-Christian, hellish near-death experience expert recently crowed that a little bit of hell is good for you! It turns your life around, he wrote.

The Christian who had the most masterful gift for horror entertainment, though, was Johnathan Edwards (1703–1758). Playful paranormalists defy funda-Christian, hellish NDExperts to try to exact as much sheer terror with their horror writing as Edwards did with his. Edwards was as scary a preacher as ever thumped a Bible, but he hardly moved a muscle, and his manner of delivery was as grave as it was solemn. One churchgoer noted that during his sermons, Edwards "looked straight forward" and that he "looked on the bell rope until he looked it off." This inspiring preacher preached so frightening a message that during one sermon, "a great moaning and crying out through the whole house could be heard," according to another reverend who was sitting in the congregation.

Johnathan Edwards and his fellow Puritan frightmongers were the literary progenitors of Stephen King and other great American masters of the horror story. All funda-Christian, hellish NDExperts ought to study Edwards's virtuoso use of the vocabulary of the alluringly unknown. He knew how to put the expressions of the ordinary language of the paranormal to work to create an atmosphere of everlasting horror. The word *strange* fascinated him.

> The bodies of the wicked, after the Resurrection, will be strange, hideous kinds of bodies; there will be a strange crew at the left hand of Christ at the Day of Judgment . . . such a strange punishment as being suitable to such a strange and monstrous evil . . . the torments being principally spiritual and consisting in the horrors of the mind makes it appear like some strange fable or dream.

Edwards adroitly marshaled the language of the paranormal to make hell "real enough to be found in the atlas." the preacher made abundant reference to the flames that always engulf the place, too, just as we have found to be characteristic of the fiery rhetoric of today's funda-Christians.

> The God that holds you over the pit of hell, much as one holds a spider, or some loathsome insect, over the

fire, abhors you, and is dreadfully provoked; his wrath towards you burns like fire; he looks upon you as worthy of nothing else, but to be cast into the fire . . . 'tis nothing but his hand that holds you from falling into the fire every moment.

Johnathan Edwards was not the first fearsome American preacher or writer of horror stories who knew how to ignite fire storms of terror with the print on a page. Before him, Cotton Mather wrote about the devil who

relishes no sacrifices like those of human heart-blood, and unto whom there is no music like the bitter, dying, doleful groans ejaculated by the roasting children of men.

There are other parallels between funda-Christian literature and horror literature, both of which, for example, are overstocked with monsters. The concept of the monstrous is compounded of several elements, such as the notion of animal ferocity. Werewolves and vampires are among the monsters of horror fiction that merge a fierce, beastly nature with a human one.

The Beast is one of the funda-Christians' favorite Biblical monsters. It's "The Beast this" and "The Beast that" every time you watch JAY-zus-vision or listen to funda-Christian radio.

Horrific unsightliness is one traditional feature of many monsters of horror fiction; they are deformed, ugly, and hideous. So you would think the devil would look a fright, but, no, to hear funda-Christians tell it, Satan is a very handsome fellow.

There are many funda-Christians who absolutely can be relied upon quickly to bring up the subject of how pretty Satan is; they emphasize it, and they dwell on it. Judging by how often they say it, one of the funda-Christians' favorite things to say about the devil is that he is the kind of guy they would find easy to look at, or would be drawn to look at, going strictly, as funda-Christians do, by the Bible's standards.

Funda-Christians are very concerned that we all hear their message about how attractive they find Satan to be, and, therefore, how much they would enjoy looking at him, or anyone would, according to their Bible beliefs. So, we kindly playful paranormalists want to get up onto our own soapboxes to help funda-Christians get this important information out. Therefore, people, please always remember: Satan is just *gorgeous,* or so funda-Christians say and believe.

You have to see the humor here. I mean, you really must try to see what is funny about all of this. But first, you must understand how it is easy to come to the conclusion that funda-Christians see Satan as beautiful in appearance.

Funda-Christians are particularly suspicious that the radiantly loving being that near-death experients meet might be the devil.

Professor Grootish, a funda-Christian philosophaster who teaches at an alleged seminary, has made a name for himself in fundamentalist circles by writing sniffy critiques of the works of us scholarly proparanormalists. He thinks the bright, loving being of light people see during peri-mortal visions is just Satan, in a flammeous overcoat.

He believes that, in addition to the regular Jesus, there is another one, an evil impostor, running around. He calls the devilish one the New Age Jesus.

Even if the loving, brilliantly illuminated Being you meet during a near-death experience introduces Himself as Jesus, and looks just like Him from the paintings, don't believe Him for a minute! You've got to put Him to the professor's ideological test, first. Jesus has to pass the professor's Bible exam before He can even be Him!

Now this is really entertaining. Fundamentalist watchers enjoy the spectacle of funda-Christians warning that the loving Christ whom near-death experients meet might be the devil. And since all playful paranormalists strive to be on friendly terms with fundamentalists, I have helpfully written out a succinct statement that funda-Christian clinicians might wish to use for advising patients who are near death.

Remember, don't approach any beautiful, loving Light you see in the near beyond. Stay back in the dark. If you are a funda-Christian, you'd better keep a safe distance from any bright, loving Light you see when you are dead or dying. If you are forced to break your silence, just say hello from Reverend Bakker and Brother Swaggart.

Are Children Being Deceived, Too?

Pediatrician Melvin Morse and other nonfunda-Christian experts have reported that children have near-death experiences, too, which brings us the question: Will there be a parallel development in hellish, funda-Christian near-death experience research? Will a funda-Christian NDExpert someday crawl out from under a Bible to compile a book of graphic case histories of critically ill little ones who were thrown into hell, horrendously scorched, toasted, and baked, frightened out of their wits, and scared almost to death, when they almost died?

The doctrine that the devil can disguise himself as Christ must be particularly troubling to fundamentalist authorities as they consider the possibilities of pediatric near-death experiences. Does God permit Satan to even fool dying kids by masquerading as Jesus? Or is God powerless to prevent that kind of Satanic deception? If so, common decency dictates that funda-Christian NDExperts urgently prepare clear, precise instructions that will enable desperately ill, dying preschoolers to distinguish a Satanophanic Jesus from the real, true funda-Christian one.

And would God allow the devil to sneak up on a dying toddler by appearing as Santa Claus or Pat Robertson, Jerry Falwell or the Easter Bunny?

Playful paranormalists are shocked by the funda-Christian NDExperts' insensitive irresponsibility in ignoring important, answerable, clinical questions like these about pediatric hellish near-death experiences. Are there large numbers of funda-Christian, hellish near-death experiences among critically ill children who almost die in hospitals? According to their theories, do the funda-Christian NDExperts expect the incidence of hellish near-death experiences to be higher among gravely ill, dying Muslim, Jewish, Hindu, Buddhist, regular Christian, or Mormon children than among gravely ill, dying funda-Christian children?

What are the aftereffects of hellish, funda-Christian peri-mortal visionary experiences of childhood? Do the little tykes have recurrent nightmares afterward, or withdraw socially, or exhibit other post-traumatic symptoms? Compared to kids whose near-death experiences are full of love and blissful inspiration, are children who have hellish near-death experiences more likely to have residual brain damage, or to become funda-Christians, as a result of their ordeal? Do troubled children with a history of fire-setting have a higher percentage of hellish experiences when they almost die than do troubled children with no history of firesetting?

I bring up this particular question because funda-Christian emphasis on infernal near-death experiences is another aspect of the paranormal's fascination with fire: Firewalking people, fireproof people, people spontaneously combusting, people condemned as witches or heretics being burned alive; people burning in the angry inner flames of funda-Christian imaginations. It is people that the paranormal enjoys seeing on fire, or being immune to it. Why no reports of spontaneous combustion of pigs, for example?

It is rare to see living human beings in flames. Few of us would ever witness the spectacle, were it not for the movies, where it is a peculiarly common sight, attesting to its inherent human interest and, for some, entertainment appeal. Funda-Christians take delight in their own inner vistas of us human beings they dislike being raked over hot, smoldering coals as, slowly, we are roasted into an anguished infinitude of misery. Funda-Christians enjoy musing on the rest of us receiving our comeuppances in the fires of hell.

Fundamentalist firebugs can't keep their minds' eyes off inward images of living people blazing up in eternal flames of burning discomfort. Anyone with psychological insight knows that in the narrow recesses of those closed funda-Christian minds, fundamentalists love watching horror movies of consciousness. They pretend they are spouting all that mindless dogma about everyone else going to hell solely out of concern for our salvation. But it is easy to grasp what is really going on. The rest of us realize that funda-Christians secretly get a kick out of imagining us nonconformists writhing our ways through an achey endlessness as we burn in hell. So playful paranormal-ists take comfort in Mark Twain's disclaimer, "Heaven for the climate, but hell for the company."

Light-Hearted People Are Entertained by Stories of Near-Death Experiences, Too

But, as I have shown earlier, it is not just the fundamen-talist who finds stories of near-death experiences entertaining. And while fundamentalists definitely favor the more horrific versions of those encounters, there are lots of peri-mortal visions that make good entertainment fare for sweet-tempered, light-hearted people, too.

The amusement appeal of near-death experiences resem-bles that of ancient periparanormal travel books about enchanting, unknown regions over the far horizon.

Television has enabled hundreds of millions of viewers worldwide to see and to hear firsthand accounts of ordinary folks who have glimpsed beautiful, light-filled realms beyond the known horizons of death. What is more, since modern medical savvy has created a pool of tens of millions of people widely dispersed over the planet who have been beyond and back, many if not most of us have a friend or relative from whom we can hear the details during a face-to-face exchange.

As a consequence, a publicly accepted vocabulary alluding to the near-beyond has been spoken and written into being. Everyone knows the import of the standard phrases; indeed, their use has become conventional: "out of the body," "the tunnel," "the light," "the life review," "the near-death experi-ence," and so on. It is as though a new vista is opening up within our collective, consciousness. Together, we are groping for the right words to bring to the situation as we piece togeth-er a new inner geography of the other side.

Our predicament is analogous to that of people of antique civilizations as they tried to make sense of travelogues of peregri-nating adventurers who probed far beyond the limits of the known world. Those ancient explorers, too, lacked appropriate literal language for describing the weird spectacles they beheld.

On that score, it was lucky that Aristeas was a poet and that he had a rich, figurative vocabulary at his disposal. In that age, and under those circumstances, encountering exotic inhabitants of unknown lands, incomprehensible customs, and bizarre technologies must have been indistinguishable from visionary voyages across the known boundaries of consciousness. Then, gradually, as centuries of accounts accumulated and were compared and cross-correlated, a coherent overall picture emerged of the regions beyond the ends of the world.

Because people who have near-death experiences can now intelligibly, and rapidly, communicate with one another about what they encounter, and can pass some sort of sense of it along to the rest of us, a consensual reality is emerging. Today, a common language of the near-death realm having become available, we are taking a collective imaginative leap across another kind of frontier. And we ordinary folk are enjoying the adventure!

This, then, is why near-death experiences entertain—and why we should pay attention to stories that entertain, just as we did in the times of Confucius and Jesus. The fact is, people enjoy trying to solve puzzles and paradoxes, just as they enjoy pushing back the limits of the known world. Near-death experiences entertain by playing to our delight in paradox; they exploit a peculiarity of the relationship between the meaning of the word death and the criteria whereby the word can be correctly applied in any given instance.

In the case of many familiar words, there seems to be no difference between the meaning of the word and the criteria for its application. For example, there doesn't seem to be any significant difference between the meaning of the word *red* and the criteria by which we determine that it is true to say a particular fire engine is red.

In the case of *dead*, though, there is a world of difference. By definition, death is a state from which one doesn't return. If a person is pronounced dead, no matter how sure the doctors were that their pronouncing it was correct, no matter how many dozens or hundreds of persons in that same condition they had pronounced dead, none of whom had ever snapped out of it; and no matter how stringently the standard medical criteria were applied, if that person subsequently resumes vital activities and regains consciousness, the logic of language still obliges us to say that person was not dead.

There is an understandable tendency to take what people who survive an ordeal like that say about death seriously, although in some respects they aren't in any better position than anyone else to talk about it, since they weren't, in fact, dead. Hence, near-death experiences engage our interest by unveiling the Zeno-logic of death: there is a point presently known as death, but if you reach it and are aware you have done so, at least if you reverse direction and come back from it, then you never were there in the first place, because by the very fact of your having reached it, it would have receded far beyond your reach to an incomprehensible distance and in an unimaginable direction.

Putting it this way exposes a frustrating unfairness of the situation. It is as though there were a stipulation that the goal post would be moved back were the athlete to reach it. This is particularly ironic in the case of those who have been declared dead and returned with wondrous tales of the beyond, for it is in large part because of their trailblazing that we can no longer call what they went through death.

So, through their near-death pioneering, a curious development has taken place unnoticed, namely, millions of people now alive have returned from a situation that a century ago was simply designated "death," and they have informed us that even after that point, they were very much alive, very acutely conscious. What is more, they say that even from within that experience they had realized there was to be a continuation of conscious existence, and that, in fact, they had already been taken up in its flow, comforted and welcomed and reunited with loved ones lost. So, by the criteria of 1890, even those of 1930, life after death has indeed been proven.

And this is the last laugh! Do you get it? All those silly big three discussers in all those silly discussions are still denying what all the world already knows!

Near-death experiences do not challenge just the rules of language; it is also a precept of the intrapsychic life that one does not return from the dead. Accordingly, round-trips to the other side defy not only linguistic conventions, but deep-seated psychological strictures as well. Because they engage us by the way they draw attention to an uncrossable boundary within ourselves, near-death experiences entertain (and this will come as a shock) in a manner analogous to that of the old-fashioned freak shows.

The uncanny unease one feels upon contemplating Siamese twins, hermaphrodites, bearded ladies, plastic people (whose skin and joints stretch far beyond the ordained limits), elephant men, frog women, giants, or midgets, represents the resurfacing of the infantile anxieties one felt one had mastered in the course of normal development. It was uncomfortable enough differentiating oneself from one's mother, self from not-self, male from female, human from animal, adult from child, though we thought we got those distinctions down at a time of our lives before most of us remember. We feel a resurgence of the old tensions in the presence of people whose very physiognomy wreaks havoc with heartfelt conventions. The strongest such distinction of all, and probably the latest to be crystallized, is the internal line separating the living from the dead.

Because they make us feel wondrously unfamiliar with that old, familiar, and steadfast distinction, near-death experiences cast an irresistible spell, weave an inescapable magic.

Enter the Greatest Attraction: Love

Near-death experiences are proof positive that the paranormal can tell a good love story, too. In my opinion, that is the main reason they have been such comforting, uplifting, and inspiring entertainment for people everywhere. The fact that love is the dominant theme of so many near-death experiences accounts for by far the greatest share of their total entertainment appeal, I believe.

Peri-mortal visionary experiences are not the only paranormal phenomena that derive entertainment value from love, however. At present, for example, the notion of being soul mates is enjoying a flurry of great favor on the paranormal scene. Many folks who are sold on the paranormal enjoy theorofantasizing about being bound to some other person, a soul mate, by a strange, metaphysical relationship of dual self-identity.

There also are many enchanting stories of people who met their true loves miraculously, or under chance circumstances so extraordinary as to seem paranormal. These happily mystical encounters often involve the phenomenon of love at first sight, a phenomenon that, because of its seeming inexplicability and spontaneity, also can suggest that it is paranormal.

Don't forget, either, that folks always have consulted fortune-tellers about affairs of the heart. The written queries uncovered at ancient oracle sites are the same questions that are familiar to roadside palm readers today.

The paranormal entertains by speculating about the metaphysics of love between soul mates, by serving as a supernatural matchmaker, and by dispensing advice to the lovelorn. The paranormal poses questions about love in its many kinds and meanings.

The love so many people feel during peri-mortal visions is agape, and agape is the essence of the entertainment appeal of most near-death experiences. The loving being of light many experients meet manifests agape, and agape is the kind of love the being of light is interested in during the experients' panoramic life reviews.

Agape is unselfish, charitable love for another. It is brotherly love in its highest manifestation. Agape is given freely and spontaneously, with no consideration of the merit of the beloved and no calculation of cost or gain to the giver. Agape is human love made in the image of divine love, the love of God or Christ for humankind.

Agape is a gala, celebrational love, too. It is festive in mood and in meaning. Early Christians applied the word to love feasts, common meals of fellowship. Agape is rich in oral satisfaction.

Agape is inspiring and uplifting, comforting and consoling. It is as close as human love gets to transcendence. The best near-death experiences draw human hearts back to agape, and that is why they are fine and lasting entertainment for people everywhere.

Many peri-mortal visions are filled with the joys of familial love, too, in visionary reunions. The rediscovery of the psychomanteion permits psychologists to recreate that essential feature of near-death experiences, and to enable bereaved people to renew bonds of love with dear ones lost to death. Perhaps by recreating the near-death experience in its entirety, we will be able to bring more agape into the world. Empathic near-death experiences are a natural pathway to that end. The way leads through love and laughter to humor and the hereafter.

Many survivors of close brushes with death remark that the loving being of light they met had a warm, vibrant sense of humor. Others recall making funny and offbeat observations even during the time medical personnel assumed they were dead. These details show that the sense of humor remains intact and active well into the advanced stages of the dying process. There can be little doubt that human beings have tempered and sweetened their musings about death and dying with generous doses of humor from a time long before history records. Near-death experiences are a pregnant source of comic themes, and to point this out is to account also for a certain discernible portion of their total entertainment appeal. Playful paranormalism proposes that understanding the near-death experience—or any other purportedly paranormal phenomenon—in its full human meaning presupposes that one grasp it in its relationship with humor. And, although it is perhaps not a theoretical prerequisite of the same, I would bet that it is at least a practical one, that one have a kind and lively sense of humor.

Playful paranormalism is the best theory for explaining peri-mortal empathic phenomena. Near-death experiences are humorological, so it is not surprising they would be transmissible. Like near-death experiences, humor is contagious.

All elementary school teachers and all comedians know that mirth is infectious. If one or two kids in a classroom begin to giggle, soon all the pupils will be. In the party game "belly laugh," participants lie on the floor linked in a human chain, with each player's head lying on the next one's abdomen. The first person in the chain to laugh sets off a wave of happy cacchination that quickly travels around the room.

Peri-mortal visions are communicable, too. Now that we know that, we can learn safely to recreate them.

For two decades now, the world has been enchanted by the words of those who returned from the brink of death with messages of hope and inspiration from a luminous realm of love and peace. It is time that we follow in their footsteps, because additional, real understanding of the near-death experience depends on our being able to recreate those sublime spiritual visions safely and reliably.

The best we can hope to come from this remarkable situation is that there is going to be the opening of a window of opportunity for love on this planet. Clinicians who make an effort to learn about shared near-death experiences will be able to aid and abet that significant opportunity. Helping professionals will be able to apply their understanding of this phenomenon to prepare relatives and friends of the terminally ill for the profound spiritual experiences in which so many of them are going to be participating. That will make it possible for myriads of people throughout the world to realize that we do not have to die to get a glimpse of the love that awaits us in the light beyond.

ABOUT THE AUTHOR

Raymond Moody is the author of seven books, including *Life After Life*, which has sold over ten million copies worldwide. He coined the phrase "near-death experience," and is recognized as the world's leading expert on the phenomenon. He is also a compelling lecturer on the subject, as well as on out-of-body experiences; the relationship of the paranormal to the performing arts; and the interconnections between humor, illness, health, and grief recovery. He has appeared on numerous national television shows, such as *Oprah, The Today Show, Turning Point,* and *Geraldo*.

Dr. Moody has a B.A., M.A., and Ph.D. from the University of Virginia, and an M.D. from the Medical College of Georgia. He is the recipient of the World Humanitarian Award in Denmark, as well as a bronze medal in the Human Relations Category at the New York Film Festival for the movie version of *Life After Life*. He is the creator of the Dr. John Dee Memorial Theater of the Mind, which enables people to experience altered states of consciousness for the purposes of education, entertainment, and spiritual advancement. Dr. Moody is the current holder of the Bigelow Chair of Consciousness Studies at the University of Nevada, Las Vegas. He and his wife, Cheryl, live and conduct research at his home in rural Alabama.

Hampton Roads Publishing Company
publishes books on a variety of subjects including
metaphysics, health, complementary medicine, visionary fiction,
and other related topics. For a copy of our latest catalog,
call toll-free (800) 766-8009, or send your name and address to

Hampton Roads Publishing Company, Inc.
134 Burgess Lane
Charlottesville, VA 22902
e-mail: hrpc@hrpub.com
www.hrpub.com